COUNSELOR WELLNESS

COUNSELOR WELLNESS

Caring for Self to Care for Others

Richard D. Parsons, Ph.D., Karen L. Dickinson, Ph.D., and Bridget Asempapa, Ph.D.

West Chester University

SAN DIEGO

Bassim Hamadeh, CEO and Publisher
Amy Smith, Senior Project Editor
Casey Hands, Associate Production Editor
Emely Villavicencio, Senior Graphic Designer
Stephanie Kohl, Licensing Coordinator
Natalie Piccotti, Director of Marketing
Kassie Graves, Vice President of Editorial
Jamie Giganti, Director of Academic Publishing

cognella® | ACADEMIC PUBLISHING
3970 Sorrento Valley Blvd., Ste. 500, San Diego, CA 92121

To the ONE who makes our lives beautiful!
To Ginny, John, Reuben and the rest of our families who balance our lives.

BRIEF CONTENTS

DETAILED CONTENTS

PREFACE

First Lady Michelle Obama, in her 2014 address to the members of the American School Counseling Association, gave voice to a reality that school counselors have long known.

> You all have one of the hardest, most stressful, most important and most underappreciated jobs of anyone in this country—and I live with the President of the United States. So frankly, when I think about what you all do on an average day, well, quite frankly, I'm amazed.

Take a moment and think about her observation: *"When I think about what you all do on an average day, ... I'm amazed."*

While her comments were addressing the role and function of one counseling specialty, it applies to all professional counselors. Yes! What we do is amazing. What we do is life-giving. What we do is, sometimes, life-saving. What we do is a gift to those we serve and a gift for those of us who are fortunate to provide such a service. It is a gift; however, it is one that can come at a cost to our well-being.

Times They Have Changed

Mental health needs in our communities, college campuses, and schools have increased to the point where the demand is at a critical level with not enough professionals available to meet this need (Weiner, 2018). One immediate effect of this increase is the unrealistic caseloads assigned to counselors at mental health services facilities, college campuses, and school counseling centers.

As if this were not enough, to signal concern for today's counselor's emotional well-being, we must add to the mix of stressors the fact that counselors will engage with clients, including children and youth, who have been exposed to traumatic events. Helping those with trauma makes counselors vulnerable to internalizing their clients' trauma and with that exposure place themselves at risk of burnout, compassion fatigue, and secondary (vicarious) traumatization. In one study, the American Counseling Association (ACA, 2010) reported that of those surveyed, more than 63% reported knowing colleagues they would consider impaired. The magnitude of the finding moved the American Counseling Association to develop a task force for the sole purpose of decreasing impairment and enhancing wellness among its members.

Caring for Self

It is clear that for counselors to be effective, they need to attend to and maintain their emotional health and well-being. This is not merely a good idea; it is an ethical mandate. The American Counseling Association's Code of Ethics, for example, clearly states in the introduction to Section C: Professional Responsibility that counselors

> *engage in self-care activities to maintain and promote their emotional, physical, mental and spiritual well-being to best meet their professional responsibilities.* (ACA, 2014)

Other professional organizations note the same concern about counselor impairment and the need for counselors to engage in wellness programming. The American School Counselor's Association is very clear on this matter, stating,

> *(School counselors) monitor their emotional and physical health and practice wellness to ensure optimal professional effectiveness. School counselors seek physical or mental health support when needed to ensure professional competence.* (ASCA, 2016, B3.f)

Sadly, it would appear that the proverb "but who is wurs shod, than the shoemaker's wyfe" (J. Heywood Dialogue of Proverbs, 1546, I, xi, E1V) applies to counselors in that they often fail to practice what they preach, especially regarding self-care.

Given the potential of harm, not only to counselors but also to those they serve, a program fostering counselor wellness is essential to preventing burnout, compassion fatigue, or secondary traumatization and ensuring ethical practice.

Counselor Wellness: Caring for Self to Care for Others is a book that provides a look at the potential dangers to one's emotional well-being that can be incurred in the process of serving as a professional counselor. In addition to reviewing the current research on burnout, compassion fatigue, and secondary trauma, *Counselor Wellness: Caring for Self to Care for Others* details steps to be taken to intervene at times of debilitating stress and strategies for reducing and preventing the deleterious effects of serving in such an essential and stress-filled role.

About the Format of This Book

Each chapter opens with a counselor's reflection. These opening reflections are used to set the stage for the content that follows. It may be helpful to return to these opening vignettes following the completion of the chapter to apply what has been learned to that scenario. Also, each chapter will provide case illustrations and guided exercises designed to make the concepts discussed come alive.

While citing the most recent research and evidence-based approaches to recognizing, intervening, and preventing threats to the counselor's emotional well-being, each chapter provides examples of lived experiences by counselors in the field.

This text, like all texts, provides an expanded knowledge base and guidance in the development of additional skills. Our hope, however, is that the material presented facilitates counselors' abilities to genuinely care for themselves so that they are better positioned to care for those in their charge.

—rdp/kld/ba 2020

REFERENCES

American Counseling Association's Taskforce on Counseling Wellness and Impairment. (2010). Retrieved from http://www.counseling.org/wellness_taskforce/index.htm

American School Counselor Association (2016). *ASCA ethical standards for school counselors*. Alexandria, VA.: Author.

Heywood, J. (1546). Dialogue of Proverbs i. xi. E1V]. Cited in Proverb Hunter. Retrieved from: http://proverbhunter.com/who-is-worse-shod-than-shoemakers-wife/

Weiner, S. (2018). Addressing the escalating psychiatrist shortage. Retrieved from: https://www.aamc.org/news-insights/addressing-escalating-psychiatrist-shortage

ACKNOWLEDGMENTS

As is true with all books, this one could not have come to fruition without the help of many besides the three of us listed as authors. Beyond the emotional support we received from our families, our loved ones who truly help balance our lives, and the insightful suggestions offered by many of our colleagues and students at West Chester University, this final product is a reflection of the support given by all at Cognella Academic Publishing. We would like to say thank you to Jamie Giganti, director of academic publishing for believing in this project; Carrie Montoya, revisions and author care manager, who was always available to guide us when we lost our way; and Amy Smith, our project manager, who certainly kept us on schedule.

Finally, a very special thank you goes out to Kassie Graves, vice president of editorial, whose creative vision, endless energy, and inspiring enthusiasm served to sustain us throughout the project. It is truly a gift to be able to work with such competent and caring individuals, without whom this project would not have been possible.

—rdp/kld/ba 2020

Counseling as a Gift and a Calling

My friends have always come to me with their problems, and I like to help people, so I think I'll be a great counselor!

—Allison, Counseling Student

❝I *like to help people."* This is quite a noble thought—one that you may have had when starting your journey to becoming a counselor. A desire to be of help to another is certainly something that would be common among those entering the counseling profession. In addition to a desire to help others, many entering the counseling profession are known as good listeners, exhibiting the abilities to understand other perspectives and engage in effective problem solving. Being a professional counselor, however, requires much more than being a good, caring listener. Walking alongside someone in a time of need is truly a gift, but it is a gift that carries a heavy responsibility. Central to that responsibility is the commitment to gaining the skill and knowledge necessary to be an ethical, effective counselor, one who recognizes the awesomeness of counseling. This chapter will address the issue of counseling as a gift and a calling. After completing the chapter, the reader will be able to complete the following:

a. Describe the elements that go into being a counselor.

b. Describe what the client and counselor may bring to the counseling relationship.

c. Explain how a counselor's identity is not one that is only evident when working but also evolves as the counselor "becomes" at work and beyond.

Gladly Going Beyond "9 to 5"

A job is something one does for a paycheck. It typically has a defined set of responsibilities, structured workplace, and specific times of engagement. A job provides one with the means to meet the essential needs of life. When applying for a job, there is often a list of criteria that is required and a description of the expected tasks to be performed, if hired. Often, those tasks are meant to be completed within a structured time frame, and when the workday is over, the job and duties are left "at the office."

The role and demands of the counselor are not as predictable and often do not fit into the constraints of a structured workday. Much is expected of one entering the profession of counseling and much is given. For those entering the profession of counseling, their "work" provides much more than a paycheck. Many who enter the counseling profession report that theirs is a "calling," a response to an internal drive and feeling, that this is what they are meant to do. Perhaps that was your experience?

What thoughts went into your decision to be a counselor? Did you think you had the skills to interpret information, develop a goal, or make someone feel comfortable and safe? Or did you wish to support someone in a time of need? Did you simply feel a desire or passion to go into counseling? No matter what may have brought you to the decision to become a counselor, entering the field of counseling invites you to find congruence, an alignment, between who you are and what you are doing. To be able to follow such a path is clearly a gift.

The "Work" to Be Done

Counselors are helpers. Counselors are often problem solvers. But counseling and the role and responsibility of one who is a counselor far exceeds the implication of these descriptors. According to the American Counseling Association (ACA), "The practice of counseling [is] to promote respect for human dignity and diversity" (ACA, Preamble, 2014). This point is made in even greater clarity when reviewing the National Association of Social Workers' (NASW) description of the charge given to its members who provide service "with particular attention to the needs and empowerment of people who are vulnerable, oppressed, and living in poverty" (NASW, 2017). It is clear that those in the counseling professions provide valuable service to their clients. It is also clear that the type of service provided can be life altering, targeting the facilitation of the health and welfare of their clients.

Role Demands

Fulfilling such challenging and responsible expectations demands more than a "9-to-5" mentality when it comes to being a counselor and doing one's "job." Counselors give much more than time and energy; they often give a piece of themselves. As described by Skovholt (2012), as counselors, "we must bring so much of our self to the meeting with our client: our emotional self, our intellectual self, our energetic self, our hopeful self, our ethical self, our knowledgeable and competent self, our sensitive self, our emotionally courageous self, our trusting self, our confident self and more and more."

The personal level of investment and involvement required of a counselor can be exhausting and even possibly detrimental to their physical and mental health. Counselors must understand what they are committing to in their role as a counselor. It is vital to not only their own well-being but also the effectiveness of the service they provide to their clients. Case Illustration 1.1 provides an example from one counselor.

CASE ILLUSTRATION 1.1

What Did I Get Into?!

All I ever wanted was to be a school counselor—help students get through the school day and give teachers strategies for behavior change. What I didn't expect was to spend 12 hours a day here at school and go home exhausted from the demands of the parents and the student issues!

This was what Molly tearfully shared when the district counselors met for our first team meeting of the school year. We affirmed to her how tiring and frustrating this job could be but asked her to remember why she became a school counselor. When she had calmed a bit, she smiled and said she wanted to be a support, a smiling face for those hurting, and someone with whom every student could feel safe. We reminded her that it takes a lot of time and emotional energy to be empathetic, to learn every student's story, and to do that in a short time frame with a myriad of other tasks to perform.

Molly said she was quite aware of all she needed to do and relapsed into tears as she said she didn't feel like she could help them all. We realized that Molly came into her position like most of us, ready to help everyone and change the world, or at least the school experience. We asked her to reflect on the time and energy she put into her role and offered to help her prioritize her tasks and her goals. With the promise of taking time to think about the best use of her time and energy, Molly smiled, and we started our meeting.

Counselors need to be aware of what it is that they are putting into and getting out of being a counselor. Exercise 1.1 provides an opportunity to do this reflection.

EXERCISE 1.1

Identifying the "Ins and Outs" of Being a Counselor

Direction: Reflect on the following questions to consider what you put into, and what you get out of, being a counselor. After you are finished, meet with a colleague or supervisor to discuss how these factors may affect you and the counseling process. Examples have been provided.

What Do I Put Into "Being A Counselor"?	Possible Advantages?	Possible Disadvantages?
Time	Increase skill	No time for self
Empathy	Understand client better	Compassion fatigue

What Do I Put Into "Being A Counselor"?	Possible Advantages?	Possible Disadvantages?

What Do I Get Out of "Being a Counselor"?	Possible Advantages?	Possible Disadvantages?
Help others	Feel good about myself	Disappointment if a client doesn't want to change

The Gifts Provided, the Challenges Faced

Whether they have chosen to talk with a counselor in response to their own felt need or have been directed to talk to a counselor, as might be the case for a student sent to the school counselor or a client who was court mandated to see a drug and alcohol counselor, clients are embarking on a relationship that will invite change to occur. Change, even when highly desired, can be difficult. Change often invokes strong feelings, including fear, anxiety, and even anger and as such may invite resistance.

We must meet clients where they are, acknowledging that they may come with low motivation, lack of knowledge, ambivalence about a helper, and lack of trust of others (Skovholt, 2012). Aligning with a client at such a time can take a toll, not only on the counseling relationship but also on the counselor. Case Illustration 1.2 provides the challenges encountered when working with one client.

CASE ILLUSTRATION 1.2

"I Don't Need Help"

Jered walked into the counselor's office with his head down. He didn't know why he was there. He was supposed to be able to handle everything by himself. Isn't that what men were supposed to do? He had everything—a family who loved him and good health. Why would he need a counselor? His breakup with his partner of 5 years had happened over 2 years ago. He should be over it, right? And why would he tell this person he didn't even know about himself?

Any time he had told anyone anything in the past, they had just said, "Suck it up." "You're fine." "You think you have problems? Let me tell you about problems." What would a counselor do that would make a difference? Jered couldn't believe he was talked into coming here. What should he say? What if he told him something, and he didn't believe him, or if he laughed, or worse, told him he didn't have problems. Then what would he do? What would happen next?

Maybe he should turn around and leave.

As illustrated in the case of Jered, clients often present with challenges that could potentially block the counseling process. Experiencing client resistance can be frustrating and blind a counselor to the "gift" that they are being afforded even when working with the most resistant client. Counselors need to move beyond the inconveniences presented to embrace and accept the gift and value of the client they are invited to serve.

As a professional counselor, you will look beyond these human frailties and life inconveniences to step into the lived experiences of your clients and position yourself to walk with them toward their desired goals. Accepting our clients as they are, and unconditionally, will result in the establishment of trust and allow the counseling process to move forward.

What a gift to be experienced. As a professional counselor, you are invited into an authentic relationship with another. The counseling relationship invites a counselor to step away from artificial roles and engage in a genuine relationship, accepting the other as a co-journeyer. Being invited to walk with another, not doing to or for, but being and doing with another who is at a point of struggle in his or her life is an honor and a gift.

The "gifts" of our profession come with a cost. As noted in his 2010 keynote address to the ACA conference, Gerald Corey (2010) stated, "There is a good deal of stress that goes, along with being a counseling professional." Counselors have to be cognizant of the sources of stress and the degree to which they are giving of themselves. Monitoring the level of self-engagement and depletion positions counselors to be ready to give to the next client while at the same time taking care of themselves. As counselors, we recognize that clients are ultimately in control of the choices they make, and we are only invited to go along on the journey, regardless of the ending.

Balancing Care of the Client With Care of Self

As noted by the Austrian psychiatrist Viktor Frankl, "What is to give light must endure burning" (1963). While we consistently attend to our clients' well-being, it is just as important for counseling practitioners to assess their own levels of well-being (Puig et al., 2012). Counselor self-care and wellness in service of ethical, effective practice are integral parts of the ACA Code of Ethics. "Counselors engage in self-care activities to maintain and promote their own emotional, physical, mental, and spiritual well-being to best meet their professional responsibilities" (ACA, C: Introduction, 2014). Concern for this balance of care was echoed in the American School Counselor Association (ASCA) Ethical Standards for School Counselors, as it states, "[School counselors] monitor their emotional and physical health and practice wellness to ensure optimal professional effectiveness" (ASCA, B.3.f, 2016).

Counselors have the challenge of joining with a client in session while remaining separate; of attaching to one client after another; and then letting each one go (Skovholt, 2005). The balance between the counselors giving of themselves in the care of their clients while maintaining their own well-being has been depicted as moving through the following four phases of the cycle of caring (Skovholt, 2005).

- *Empathic attachment phase.* The counselor empathizes with the client and forms a personal bond of trust with him or her.

- *Active involvement phase.* The counselor dives into the client's problems and works with him or her on them.

- *Felt separation phase.* The counselor experiences the end of a human relationship and reaffirms his or her own identity and separation from that of the client.

- *Re-creation phase.* The counselor is reenergizing the self to enter enthusiastically into another cycle of bonding and separation with the next client.

Maintaining a healthy balance between the sharing of self in the service of another and in caring for oneself is not always easy. The counseling relationship is intimate. It is an intense interaction between two individuals and it is one that can arouse emotions in both the client and the counselor. In a process that has been termed transference, a client may redirect feelings, desires, and even expectations onto the counselor. The time and energy expended by a counselor in the process of counseling may also produce a situation of countertransference in which the counselor's feelings and desires surface and may take form in the counseling interaction. The counselor has to find a balance between his or her emotional involvement and the ability to gain emotional distance for the client's needs to be met (Caliso & Lee, 1983).

Professional Identity as Personal Identity

Those entering a profession, such as counseling, often report feeling an internal drive or feeling directing them in this vocational path. Those with such a calling "know" it is what they are meant to do. Entering the field of counseling invites one to find congruence, an alignment between who they are and what they are doing.

One cannot separate the professional identity of a counselor from his or her personal identity. As counselors grow in the profession, they grow in their counselor identities, moving from "doing" counseling to "being" counselors.

Consider the following. You are in a situation in which you have been working with a client who is very upset about failing to get a promotion. You are empathic to your client and able to convey empathic understanding and nonjudgmental acceptance. Contrast this with your response to a colleague who is upset about not receiving the recognition she desired when your opinion was that she simply did not work hard enough to gain that recognition. Can you be as empathic in your understanding? Or consider a situation in which you are a school counselor, able to understand and support a new student's sadness resulting from the family's move which has now negatively affected her grades. Can you convey that understanding and support when your own child has difficulty completing his homework because of his disappointment from being cut from the football team? Are you truly "being" a counselor if you only use your counseling skills, your counseling values, and your counseling orientation when stepping into your formal role as counselor? Being a counselor is a reflection of one's identity; doing counseling is a process engaging knowledge and skills, and with time, the two become one.

EXERCISE 1.2

Being a Counselor Full Time

Directions: Read the following situations and consider your reaction to each within the three different settings. Reflect on what your thoughts, feelings, and behaviors would be and try to identify what may be triggers for which you will need to be aware. It may be helpful to discuss your responses with a colleague or supervisor. An example has been provided.

Situation	At Work (Client or Student)	At Home (Family Member)	With Friends	Trigger?
A group/team or family member does not do her share	Feeling: I feel frustrated. Thought: I think the directions may not be explicit. Behavior: I will go over the directions again.	Feeling: I feel angry. Thought: I think she never does her share. Behavior: I won't talk to her, and it just won't get done.	Feeling: I feel frustrated. Thought: I want to remain friends, so I'll let it go. Behavior: I'll do it myself, so we can move on.	High expectations, particularly for family. When they are not met, I am angry and not forgiving.
Someone is late for an appointment/date	Feeling: Thought: Behavior:	Feeling: Thought: Behavior:	Feeling: Thought: Behavior:	
Someone disagrees with your perspective	Feeling: Thought: Behavior:.	Feeling: Thought: Behavior:	Feeling: Thought: Behavior:	

Situation	At Work (Client or Student)	At Home (Family Member)	With Friends	Trigger?
Someone provides false information on a job application	Feeling:	Feeling:	Feeling:	
	Thought:	Thought:	Thought:	
	Behavior:	Behavior:	Behavior:	
Other	Feeling:	Feeling:	Feeling:	
	Thought:	Thought:	Thought:	
	Behavior:	Behavior:	Behavior:	

As you completed Exercise 1.2, did you notice if there was a difference in how you feel, think, or act depending on the setting and your role? As a counselor, should there be a difference in how you proceed if someone provides false information on a job application? How about if that person is your client and is an undocumented immigrant? Or if that person is a good friend who is in dire straits financially? Hopefully, you can identify the meaning behind the differences so that you are prepared to be an effective and ethical counselor in your helping relationships and beyond.

Being a counselor is not just the acquisition of knowledge or the development of skills. Being a counselor encompasses a way of using your skills, your genuineness, and your empathy, as well as relying on your ethical codes when maintaining a healthy self—one that can serve others. Sound like a tall order?! It is and rightfully so when you consider the gift you are given when a client walks through your door. To view one counselor's experience of this gift, see Case Illustration 1.3.

CASE ILLUSTRATION 1.3

Truly a Gift

I remember sitting with the faculty on stage watching the students rise and receive their diplomas. As each approached, I silently reflected on my encounters with them. Each reflection brought a smile, but one almost brought me to tears.

Alex and I met quite a bit during his last two years of high school. The summer before his junior year, his mother died in a car accident that also left his father with physical limitations and unable to work. Alex was a student who, prior to the accident, wanted to become a psychologist. Following the accident, Alex found himself tending to his father and watching his 8-year-old sister. For several months, he took on the role of "man" of the house. He took a job with an industrial cleaning company and worked each night from 7 p.m. to midnight cleaning local office buildings.

When school started again in the fall, he would wake each morning, get his father set for the day, and then get both his sister and himself to school. Needless to say, his grades began to suffer, and his hopes of college and graduate school quickly faded. The decline in his academics, along with the fact that teachers noticed his loss of weight and apparent fatigue, resulted in him being referred to me, the school counselor.

Arrangements were made to have Alex and his sister move in with his maternal grandparents who lived in a neighboring district, yet they were allowed to stay in their schools in our district. I've never experienced a child with such maturity and drive while facing so many hardships. To see him now, approaching the stage not only to receive his diploma but also to be awarded a full scholarship to our state university was the best "gift" I've received in all of the years I've worked as a school counselor. Not all my work has resulted in such grand results, but as I viewed the bright, smiling faces approaching the stage, I realized that each of those students with whom I had the honor to work truly gifted me by inviting me to share in their unfolding stories.

KEYSTONES

- Being a counselor can be intense and exhausting; however, it is also a gift to be able to walk alongside someone in a time of need.

- As counselors, we bring much to our counseling relationships, "such as our emotional self, ... our ethical self, our knowledgeable and competent self, ... and more" (Skovholt, 2012).

- Counselors can embrace and accept the gift presented by clients and students, knowing that they come with many vulnerabilities.

- To help keep a balance of how much we give of ourselves, counselors may use the cycle of caring (Skovholt, 2005) to remind us that we attach to clients and then have to let go.

- An ethical, effective counselor cannot separate his or her professional identity from his or her personal identity; thus, as we grow in our counselor identity, we move from "doing" to "being."

ADDITIONAL RESOURCES

In Print

Florio, C. (2010). *Burnout & compassion fatigue: A guide for mental health professionals and care givers*. Lexington, KY: CreateSpace Independent Publishing Platform.

Parsons, R. D., & Dickinson, K. L. (2017). *Ethical practice in the human services: From knowing to being*. Thousand Oaks, CA: Sage Publications.

Skovholt, T. M., & Trotter-Mathison, M. (2016). *The resilient practitioner: Burnout and compassion, fatigue prevention and self-care strategies for the helping professions* (3rd ed.). New York, NY: Routledge.

Web Based

ACA https://www.counseling.org/

ASCA https://www.schoolcounselor.org/

Forester-Miller, H., & Davis, T. E. (2016). *Practitioner's guide to ethical decision making.* Retrieved from https://www.counseling.org/knowledge-center/ethics/ethical-decision-making

Lawson, G. (2018). *From the president: Cultivating a passion for counseling and self-care.* Retrieved from https://ct.counseling.org/2018/04/from-the-president-cultivating-a-passion-for-counseling-and-self-care/

REFERENCES

American Counseling Association (ACA). (2014). *ACA code of ethics.* Washington, DC: Author.

American School Counselor Association (ASCA). (2016). *ASCA ethical standards for school counselors.* Alexandria, VA: Author.

Caliso, J. A., & Lee, S. (1983). *Ethical issues in the patient-therapist relationship.* Retrieved from https://eric.ed.gov/contentdelivery/servlet/ERICServlet?accno=ED244219

Corey, G. (2010). *Creating your professional path: Lessons from my journey.* Alexandria, VA: American Counseling Association.

Frankl, V. (1963). *Man's search for meaning.* Retrieved from https://quotecatalog.com/quote/viktor-frankl-what-is-to-give-8abNXja/

National Association of Social Workers (NASW). (2017). *NASW code of ethics.* Washington, DC: Author. Retrieved from https://www.socialworkers.org/About/Ethics/Code-of-Ethics/Code-of-Ethics-English

Puig, A., Baggs, A., Mixon, K., Park, Y. M., Kim, B. Y., & Lee, S. M. (2012). Relationship between job burnout and personal wellness in mental health professionals. *Journal of Employment Counseling, 49*(3), 98–109.

Skovholt, T. M. (2005). The cycle of caring: A model of expertise in the helping professions. *Journal of Mental Health Counseling, 27*(1), 82–93.

Skovholt, T. M. (2012). The counselor's resilient self. *Turkish Psychological Counseling and Guidance Journal, 4*(38), 137–146.

A Gift With Challenge

How do I meet the needs of ALL students, when there are 550 of them and just one me? I love my job, but I can't do it all!

—Janice, School Counselor

I t has been established in the previous chapter that partnering with people during their most vulnerable stage of finding resolutions to any mental or behavioral health problem is a blessing and a gift! Nevertheless, it is a gift with a challenge!

Research (e.g., Lent, 2010) finds that counselors, regardless of their work settings or specialties, are generally satisfied with their profession, seeing it as not merely a job but a "calling." Even though counselors find their work rewarding, they experienced increased stress resulting from heavy caseloads, added paperwork, and increased micromanagement.

As counselors, we may be "invited" to work with clients who are unmotivated and even resistant to engaging. Perhaps resistant clients were mandated to come to counseling or are simply not fully aware of the need and value of counseling. Moreover, there are others with whom we will work with that trigger our emotional issues and stimulate countertransference. There will be times and conditions under which we will be challenged to maintain professional boundaries and professional identities (Gale & Austen, 2003; Mellin, Hunt, & Nichols, 2011).

This current chapter discusses potential costs and challenges that can be experienced as a professional counselor—challenges that can, at times, impede one's ability to appreciate the gift that makes the profession appealing. After reading this chapter, the reader should be able to complete the following:

a. Explain the prevalence of mental and behavioral health issues with an emphasis on limited human resources to address the issues.

b. Describe the various complex health conditions from a counseling perspective.

c. Describe the influence of increased global crises and their impact on professional counselors.

    d. Describe the responsibilities of a professional counselor and the inherent challenges associated with the duties.

Increasing Demand-Dwindling Resources

The demand for mental health services is on the increase. According to the National Alliance on Mental Health (2019), 1 in 5 adults in the United States experience mental illnesses, and about 1 in 25 do experience serious mental illnesses in a given year that significantly impede their involvement in significant life events.

    In the same report, it states that 1 in 5 youth ages 13–18 encounter significant mental health crises. The global prevalence of mental health problems affecting children and adolescents is 10%–20% (Kieling, 2011). This becomes especially concerning when placed against the data that shows that suicide in the United States is the second-leading cause of death among youth ages 10–34 (Centers for Disease Control and Prevention [CDC], 2019a) and that the majority of youth with suicidal behaviors have preexisting mental health disorder (Nock et al., 2013).

    It would appear that this increase is not merely an aberration but rather a signal of an emerging trend. The 2017 U.S. Census Bureau (2019) reported that the poverty rate was 12.3% and that about 39.7 million people live in poverty, a condition that contributes to not only impaired physical health but also emotional well-being. In addition, our culture is seeing increased cases of domestic violence, abuse (National Coalition Against Domestic Violence, n.d.), and suicide (CDC, 2019a).

    While the demand for mental health services is apparent, studies have shown that reduced availability of service providers has resulted in many consumers experiencing unmet mental health treatment (Han, Compton, Blanco, & Colpe, 2017). A recent study by the Health Resources and Services Administration (HRSA, 2019) indicated that shortages in mental health providers have a significant effect on meeting behavioral and mental health demand in the nation. The report showed shortages in every state. About 112 million Americans are living in mental health professional shortage areas. Six mental health professions (psychiatrists; clinical, counseling, and school psychologists; substance abuse and behavioral disorder counselors; mental health and substance abuse social workers; mental health counselors; and school counselors) absorb the increased needs, but there are projected shortages by 2025 (HRSA, 2015).

    These projected shortages present not only a challenge to the well-being of those being served but also have a significant effect on the well-being of the counselors attempting to provide needed services. Excessive caseloads affect a counselor's ability to provide quality care (Hoge et al., 2013). For example, while the ASCA (2012) recommends a 1:250 school counselor to students ratio; the reality of the limited number of school counselors and increasing demands for their services makes this ratio merely aspirational (Baker & Gerler, 2008; Lent, 2010; McCarthy, Kerne, Calfe, Lambert, & Guzman, 2010). This issue of work overload is important, especially when considering service effectiveness. As noted by Schmidt (2008), "The number of counselors hired in a school counseling program makes a difference in the quantity and quality of services offered" (Schmidt, 2008, p. 100). While speaking specifically about school counselors, Schmidt's (2008) observation is a warning about the effect on services offered by all counselors who are stretched thin. The case of Janice (Case Illustration 2.1), the school counselor, highlights some of the challenges school counselors may face.

CASE ILLUSTRATION 2.1

Janice, the School Counselor

I have been working as a school counselor for about 12 years. I started my career as a long-term substitute, and it evolved into a full-time school counselor position within a year. Throughout this period, I have worked in only elementary schools. Currently, I serve two elementary schools, and the distance between the two schools is about 15 miles. To establish consistency, I'm in one school on Monday and Tuesday, and Thursday and Friday, I'm in the other school. I have reserved Wednesdays for what I call "my curveball day." Depending on what the needs are in a particular school, I'm able to spend an additional day resolving the issues.

In my role, I serve about 550 students. The students' needs are so varied that I never know what to expect; each day is very different! They are at the formative age, and they always need emotional support. At this age, they are learning to social-ize outside of the home environment, so it is critical to provide emotional support when they need it. However, I can't do it alone! Even after gaining support from the community mental health agency that is providing a school-based therapist who vis-its each of my schools on my off days and also having a school social worker, it still feels overwhelming!

How do I meet the needs of ALL students when there are 550 of them and only one of me? I love my job, but I can't do it all!

The experience of too few resources and too much demand is not confined to our K–12 schools. College counselors, community mental health counselors, family ther-apists, and addiction counselors are similarly feeling the pressure of too much to do. For example, some college counseling centers usually have wait-lists, especially by midsemester, and some college counselors are also engaged in service-oriented activi-ties in the university community. Addiction counselors are inundated given the uptick in the opioid crisis (HRSA, 2019). As the demand grows, factors such as low salaries, constricted Medicare reimbursements, and burnout are contributing to an increasing shortage of professionals (Hoge et al., 2013).

Not Just More—but More Complex

Counselors working in the 21st century are not merely seeing more clients; they are seeing clients who are presenting with more complex and complicated issues, including comorbid or co-occurring mental health issues, conditions exacerbated by biological/ somatic factors, and those struggling to become free from significant trauma.

Cases being seen by counselors have become more complicated by the inclusion of numerous concurring biological or physical and mental health issues. Poor or ill health has exacerbated mental health disorders in many consumers. According to the Center for Chronic Disease Prevention and Health Promotion (2019b), 6 in 10 Americans live with chronic diseases, such as cardiovascular diseases, diabetes, and cancer. Research has also shown that the management of these diseases affects patients' mental health (Frasure-Smith & Lespérance, 2006; Goldney, Phillips, Fisher, & Wilson, 2004).

Counselors are experiencing clients who present with comorbid conditions, which can compound the nature of the treatment plans developed. Depression and anxiety, for example, are the two mental health disorders that have high levels of concurrent or sequential comorbidity. Although studies have found that anxiety often precedes depression (e.g., Avenevoli, Stolar, Li, Dierker, & Merikangas, 2001; Pine, Cohen, Gurley, Brook, & Ma, 1998), it often goes unrecognized and untreated because of its comorbidity with depression (Hirschfeld, 2001). In addition, clients presenting with anxiety or depression may also present with other severe mental health disorders, including trauma (O'Donnell, Creamer, & Pattison, 2004), addiction (Akin & Iskender, 2011; Volkow, 2004), and eating disorders (Braun, Sunday, Halmi, 1994). Such comorbidity places additional stress on counselors to be trained appropriately, often in diverse specialty areas, and to be competent in a variety of treatment modalities.

Challenges to Providing Service

While it is clear that the need for counseling services is great, it is also clear that there are barriers to gaining access to those services that exist and barriers to those seeking to provide service. For those seeking service, stigmatization remains one of the significant sociocultural factors that inhibit consumers' access to mental health treatment. In addition, restriction by insurance or funding sources might deter people from seeking early intervention when it is most needed. Oversight by third-party payers and the restriction imposed on the number of sessions that they will reimburse often interferes with the counselor's freedom to engage in the implementation of the desired treatment plan. However, insurance and third-party payers are not the only challenges to providing service. As seen in Case Illustration 2.2, the challenge to the provision of service may stem from the multiplicity of issues presented and the limited resources available to the client and counselor.

CASE ILLUSTRATION 2.2

What Is More Pressing?

Mercy, a first-year licensed professional counselor working for the local hospital's mental health department, was introduced to Janet, age 16, as a result of Janet's mother's concern for her well-being. Janet was brought to the emergency room by her mother after it was discovered that Janet had been "cutting."

During Janet's intake, Mercy learned additional information that complicated issues. First, she learned that Janet was pregnant as a result of being raped by a trusted family member. Janet blamed herself for the abuse. As a result of this guilt, she found herself unable to tell her mother. Janet also shared her anxiety about the fact that her parents were in the process of getting a divorce and that her grandmother was just diagnosed with stage four pancreatic cancer. It just seemed to Janet that her life was falling apart. To further complicate issues, Janet was medically diagnosed with lupus.

Janet was certainly addressing multiple issues that collectively appeared to be overwhelming her ability to cope. As a therapist, Mercy wanted to ensure that she was addressing the most significant presenting problem, which, for Janet, was her pregnancy. While the pregnancy was a pressing issue, it could not be viewed in isolation from the other major life stressors being encountered. For Mercy, the challenges appeared numerous, and her concern was where and how to start? "What is more pressing?"

Counseling in a Stressful World

Counselors of the 21st century will be confronted by those whose lives have been thrown into turmoil by local, regional, national, and international events. Wars, political unrest, and economic destabilization around the world have not only negatively affected the livelihood of the citizens of such countries but also resulted in their presence on our shores seeking asylum.

Since the passage of Section 207 of the Immigration and Nationality Act in the United States in 1980, more than three million refugees have been admitted, and more than 683,000 individuals have been granted asylum status (U.S. Department of State, n.d). The same report indicates that the United States expects to resettle about 30,000 refugees in 2019. Other countries such as Turkey, Greece, Malta, and Italy in the United Nations Economic and Social Commission for Asia and the Pacific have also witnessed a high influx of refugees (Hebebrand et al., 2016).

It is a known fact that most refugees experience some form of trauma preflight, during flight, or postflight to other countries for resettlement (Hebebrand et al., 2016; Lindert, Carta, Schafer, & Mollica, 2016), and this trauma compounds their ability to adapt and function within this new land.

The nature of the trauma is broad and impacting. Prior to the flight, some may be subjected to food insecurity, malnutrition, property loss, rape, violence of all forms, imprisonment persecution, humiliation, or torture; gender-based violence; human rights violations; or significant losses, such as the murder of family and friends (Lindert et al., 2016, p. 374). The predicament of the unknown conditions during the flight and in some cases witnessing the loss of loved ones increases the exposure to trauma. Unfortunately, their expectations are often unmet when they arrive at their resettlement. For instance, results from a study conducted with 135 English-speaking Somali adolescents who had resettled in the United States indicated that postresettlement stressors, acculturative stressors, and perceived discrimination were associated with greater post-traumatic stress disorder (PTSD) symptoms after accounting for trauma, demographic, and immigration variables (Ellis, MacDonald, Lincoln, & Cabral, 2008). The evidence is sufficient to show that the overall mental health conditions of refugees are concerning, with reports of PTSD, depression, and anxiety (Bogic, Njoku, & Priebe, 2015).

> It might be timely to modify services and introduce a refugee-informed approach in interventions that realize the widespread trauma exposure before, during and after flight and the living conditions in the host country and its impact on mental health, and respond to these needs by fully integrating knowledge about human rights violations and effects of humiliation into interventions. (Lindert et al., 2016, p. 374)

The intensity of the issues they bring to counselors presents not only a challenge to the development and implementation of effective evidence-based, trauma-informed interventions but also challenges the counselor's ability to avoid vicarious trauma, burnout, and compassion fatigue. Most of these topics that may negatively affect the professional counselor during his or her work with consumers will be addressed thoroughly in subsequent chapters of this book. Nonetheless, Case Illustration 2.3 sheds light on some of the potential challenges a counselor is likely to encounter when working with a refugee or immigrant families.

CASE ILLUSTRATION 2.3

This Is a Heavy One!

Philomena is a member of the child and adolescent treatment unit at a mental health clinic. She has been practicing for 2 years as a licensed professional counselor. As part of a long tradition at this agency, members of the unit met biweekly to discuss cases that are challenging. Starting with a big sigh, Philomena began her case presentation. "This is a heavy one!"

"My client is a 10-year-old Syrian refugee who recently resettled in the U.S. with her mother and her two younger siblings. They currently live with the mother's brother who resettled in the U.S. 2 years before their arrival. She attended one of the local public schools and was referred by her school counselor. During my first session, I met with the girl, her mother, and a translator who happens to be her mother's friend. They reported that the client is struggling to fit in with her peers, cries uncontrollably when she has to go to school, isolates from her peers when she eventually gets to school, and seems extremely fearful of adult males. According to the mother, the four of them moved into a Syrian refugee camp, following the destruction of their house and the death of her husband and eldest son. The mother reported that the camp was violent and that both she and her children experienced random 'beatings' at the hands of the leaders of the camp. She noted that such violence was commonplace and typically targeted women and female children.

"Sadly, her mother seems to be struggling as much as her daughter because of the traumatic experiences. Moreover, the whole family seems to be struggling with cultural differences and is skeptical of people in their current neighborhood. While the mother has agreed to have her child continue with counseling, she refuses to see any therapist for herself. It appears she is struggling with her issues as she kept crying uncontrollably when she narrated their story. The traumatic history this family has endured, the strangeness of this new culture, the fragility of mom and daughter, and my cultural worldview are making this a difficult case for me. Needless to say, I am open to suggestions."

A Profession With Extreme Responsibility

Most counselors are drawn to the profession because of an innate or external motivation to help others. While such a motive is noble, many enter the profession with an unrealistic understanding or appreciation of the enormity of the responsibility entrusted to them by others. Skovholt and McCarthy (1988) indicate that it is our glamorized perception of the profession as lay helpers that prevents us from appreciating the responsibility with which counselors embrace their professional duties. The power of walking with people during the time of their struggles (i.e., empathy) and the expectation of knowing what to do and how to do it (i.e., case conceptualization and treatment planning) are elements of the profession that can take their toll on the well-being of the counselor. As noted earlier, clients often present with tragic and complex experiences and are turning to the counselor in hopes, and perhaps with the expectation, of finding a path to a more desired life. While counselors understand that they are not the magic answer, nor do they have the sole responsibility to "save" the client, the realization of the degree of trust and vulnerability that a client brings to counseling highlights the responsibility we have embraced and increases the stress counselors experience in the performance of their duties.

One size does not fit all when it comes to counseling. As a result, counselors must have the ability to not only "hear" the client but also experience the story and the life being shared by the client. To be effective, a counselor needs a deep understanding of the client's situation and at times experience: "Not the equivalent of longevity, seniority, or the simple passage of time … [but] living through actual situations in such a way that it informs the practitioner's perception and understanding of all subsequent situations" (Benner & Wrubel, 1982, p. 28). This intensity can be a challenge to a counselor's well-being.

As counselors, we have much to offer. It is also true that for our effectiveness and well-being, we need to manage the boundaries that define what we do and how we do it. In the following exercise, you are invited to examine the scenarios presented and reflect on the specific challenges each case might pose to you as a counselor.

EXERCISE 2.1

What Is Our Responsibility as Counselors?

Directions: In the following exercise, we invite you to read the scenarios presented and critically establish what your role as a counselor is. Identify what the limitations are and delineate what you might do to begin to address the situation.

Note: Some of these issues are current societal issues. Additional rows have been provided for your reflection on personal, professional, and societal situations you have encountered. Take some time to decide what you might do and what your limitations are.

Scenario	What Might You Do?	What Are the Limitations?
There are increased reports of gun violence in the United States. Some reports blame mental illness and hatred and feel gun control is not needed. You are a counselor, and research has indicated that only a few mental health disorders have associated violent tendencies. You feel it is unfair to individuals with mental health issues to be clustered as violent, and you feel strongly that there is a need for you or the counseling profession to speak up!		
You are temporarily living with your mother-in-law, who lives with an 8-year-old child. The child is not a relative. However, you have noticed that the child is fed once a day.		
You overheard a conversation between your principal and one of the teachers in your school. The principal stated, "These Mexicans from godforsaken holes need to go! I do not want them in my school!"		
You are working with a client who has identified as gay. You have concerns about working with this population because it is forbidden within your culture.		

KEYSTONES

- Being a counselor is a blessing and a gift, but it comes with inherent challenges.

- Counselors working in the 21st century are not merely seeing more clients; they are seeing clients who are presenting with more complex and complicated issues, including comorbid or co-occurring mental health issues.

- Mental health is not just limited to our local or national community; it is present all around the world.

- While the demand for mental health services is apparent, reduced availability of service providers has resulted in many consumers experiencing unmet mental health treatment (Han et al., 2017), counselors managing increased caseloads, and professional counselors dealing with resultant stress.

- The power of walking with another person during a time of his or her struggles (i.e., empathy) and the expectation of knowing what to do and how to do it (i.e., case conceptualization and treatment planning) are elements of the profession that can take their toll on the well-being of the counselor.

ADDITIONAL RESOURCES

In Print

Blackwell, D. (2005). *Counseling and psychotherapy with refugees*. Philadelphia, PA: Jessica Kingsley Publishers.

Gale, A. U., & Austin, B. D. (2003). Professionalism's challenges to professional counselors' collective identity. *Journal of Counseling & Development, 81*, 3–10.

Pearlman, L. A., & Caringi, J. (2009). Living and working self-reflectively to address vicarious trauma. In C. A. Courtois & J. D. Ford (Eds.), *Treating complex traumatic stress disorders: An evidence-based guide* (pp. 202–224). New York, NY: Guilford Press.

Saakvitne, K. W., Pearlman, L. A., & the Staff of the Traumatic Stress Institute. (1996). *Transforming the pain: A workbook on vicarious traumatization*. New York, NY: W.W. Norton.

Web Based

Hoge, M. A., Stuart, G. W., Morris, J., Flaherty, M. T., Paris, M. & Goplerud, E. (2013). Mental health and addiction workforce development: Federal leadership is needed to address the growing crisis. *Health Affairs, 32* (11). doi.org/10.1377/hlthaff.2013.0541

Kaiser Family Foundation. (2019). Mental health care health professional shortage areas (HPSAs). Retrieved from https://www.kff.org/other/state-indicator/mental-health-care-health-professional-shortage-areas-hpsas/?currentTimeframe=0&sortModel=%7B%22colId%22:%22Location%22,%22sort%22:%22asc%22%7D

U.S. Department of State. (n.d.). Refugee admissions. Retrieved from https://www.state.gov/refugee-admissions/

REFERENCES

Akin, A., & Iskender, M. (2011). Internet addiction and depression, anxiety, and stress. *International Online Journal of Educational Sciences, 3*(1), 138–148.

American School Counselor Association (ASCA). (2012). *The ASCA national model: A framework for school counseling programs* (3rd ed.). Alexandria, VA: Author.

Avenevoli, S., Stolar, M., Li, J., Dierker, L., & Merikangas, K. R. (2001). Comorbidity of depression in children and adolescents: Models and evidence from a prospective high-risk family study. *Biological Psychiatry, 49,* 1071–1081.

Baker, S. B., & Gerler, E. R., Jr. (2008). *School counseling for the 21st century* (5th ed.). Columbus, OH: Pearson.

Benner, P., & Wrubel, J. (1982). Skilled clinical knowledge: The value of perceptual awareness, part 2. *Journal of Nursing Administration, 12,* 28–33.

Bogic, M., Njoku, A., & Priebe, S. (2015). Long-term mental health of war-refugees: A systematic literature review. *BMC International Health and Human Rights, 15*(29), 1–41. 10.1186/s12914-015-0064-9

Braun, D. L., Sunday S. R., Halmi K. A. (1994). Psychiatric comorbidity in patients with eating disorders. *Psychological Medicine, 24,* 859–67.

Centers for Disease Control and Prevention (CDC). (2019a). Ten leading causes of death and injury. Retrieved from https://www.cdc.gov/injury/wisqars/Leading-Causes.html

Center for Chronic Disease Prevention and Health Promotion. (2019b). Emergency preparedness for people with chronic diseases. Retrieved from https://www.cdc.gov/chronicdisease/index.htm

Ellis, H. B., MacDonald, H. Z., Lincoln, A. K., & Cabral, H. J. (2008). Mental health of Somali adolescent refugees: The role of trauma, stress, and perceived discrimination. *Journal of Counseling and Clinical Psychology, 76*(2), 184–193. 10.1037/0022-006X.76.2.184

Frasure-Smith, N., & Lespérance, F. (2006). Recent evidence linking coronary heart disease and depression. *Canadian Journal of Psychiatry, 51,* 730–737.

Gale, A. U., & Austin, B. D. (2003). Professionalism's challenges to professional counselors' collective identity. *Journal of Counseling & Development, 81,* 3–10.

Goldney, R. D., Phillips, P. J., Fisher, L. J., & Wilson, D. H. (2004). Diabetes, depression, and quality of life: A population study. *Diabetes Care, 27,* 1066–1070.

Han, B., Compton, W. M., Blanco, C., & Colpe, L. J. (2017). Prevalence, treatment, and unmet treatment needs of U.S. adults with mental health and substance use disorders. *Health Affairs, 36*(10), 1739–1747. doi:10.1377/hlthaff.2017.0584

Hebebrand, J., Anagnostopoulos, D., Eliez, S., Linse, H., Pejovic-Milovancevic, M., & Klasen, H. (2016). A first assessment of the needs of young refugees in Europe: What mental health professionals need to know. *European Child Adolescent Psychiatry, 25*, 1–6. 10.1007/s00787-015-0807-0

Health Resources and Services Administration (HRSA), U.S. Department of Health & Human Services. (2019). Designated health professional shortage areas statistics: Designated HPSA quarterly summary. Retrieved from file:///C:/Users/bbyan/AppData/Local/Packages/Microsoft.MicrosoftEdge_8wekyb3d8bbwe/TempState/Downloads/BCD_HPSA_SCR50_Qtr_Smry%20(1).pdf

Health Resources and Services Administration/National Center for Health Workforce Analysis; Substance Abuse and Mental Health Services Administration/ Office of Policy, Planning, and Innovation. (2015). *National Projections of Supply and Demand for Behavioral Health Practitioners: 2013–2025.* Rockville, Maryland: Author. Retrieved from https://bhw.hrsa.gov/sites/default/files/bhw/ health-workforce-analysis/research/projections/behavioral-health2013-2025.pdf

Hirschfeld, R.M.A. (2001). The comorbidity of major depression and anxiety disorders: Recognition and management in primary care. *The Primary Care Companion to The Journal of Clinical Psychiatry, 3*(6), 244–254.

Hoge, M. A., Stuart, G. W., Morris, J., Flaherty, M. T., Paris, M. & Goplerud, E. (2013). Mental health and addiction workforce development: Federal leadership is needed to address the growing crisis. *Health Affairs, 32*(11). Retrieved from https:// doi.org/10.1377/hlthaff.2013.0541

Kieling, C., Baker-Henningham, H., Belfer, M., Conti, G., Ertem, I., Omigbodun, O., Rohde, LA., et al. (2011). Child and adolescent mental health worldwide: Evidence for action. *Lancet, 378*, 1515–1525.

Lent, J. (2010). Stressors and stress management of counselors: Findings from interviews of professional counselors. Retrieved from http://counselingoutfitters. com/vistas/vistas10/Article_73.pdf

Lindert, J., Carta, M. G., Schafer, I., & Mollica, R. F. (2016). Refugees mental health: A public health challenge. *The European Journal of Public Health, 26*(3), 374–375.

McCarthy, C., Van Horn, V., Calfa, N. A., Lambert, R. G., & Guzman, Michele. (2010). An exploration of school counselors' demands and resources: Relationship to stress, biographic, and caseload characteristics. *Professional School Counseling, 13*(3), 146–158.

Mellin, E. A., Hunt, B., & Nichols, L. M. (2011). Counselor professional identity: Findings and implications for counseling and interprofessional collaboration. *Journal of Counseling & Development, 89*, 140–147.

National Alliance on Mental Health (2019). Prevalence of mental illness. Retrieved from https://www.nami.org/learn-more/mental-health-by-the-numbers

National Coalition Against Domestic Violence, (n.d.). Statistics. Retrieved from https://ncadv.org/statistics

Nock, M. K., Green, J. G., Hwang, I., McLaughlin, K. A., Sampson, N. A., Zaslavsky, A. M., & Kessler, R. C. (2013). *JAMA Psychiatry, 70*(3), 300–310. doi:10.1001/2013.jamapsychiatry.55

O'Donnell, M. L., Creamer, M., & Pattison, P. (2004). Posttraumatic stress disorder and depression following trauma: Understanding comorbidity. *American Journal of Psychiatry, 161*(8), 1390–1397.

Pine, D. S., Cohen, P., Gurley, D., Brook, J., & Ma, Y. (1998). The risk for early-adulthood anxiety and depressive disorders in adolescents with anxiety and depressive disorders. *Archives of General Psychiatry, 55*, 56–64.

Schmidt, J. J. (2008). *Counseling in schools* (5th ed.). Boston, MA: Pearson.

Skovholt, T. M., & McCarthy, P. R. (Eds.). (1988). Critical incidents in counselor development [special issue]. *Journal of Counseling and Development, 67*, 69–135.

U.S. Census Bureau. (2019). Income and poverty in the United States: 2017. Retrieved from https://www.census.gov/library/publications/2018/demo/p60-263.html

U.S. Department of State. (n.d.). Refugee admissions. Retrieved from https://www.state.gov/refugee-admissions/

Volkow, N. D. (2004). The reality of comorbidity: Depression and drug abuse. *Biological Psychiatry, 56*(10), 714–717. doi.org/10.1016/j.biopsych.2004.07.007

3

Loss of Professional Objectivity

I can't let it go. Where is she sleeping? Who is watching over her? Maybe, I should bring her home with me.

—Amanda, Domestic Abuse Counselor

Interacting with individuals who are facing very real and often very tragic circumstances is part of the job of being a counselor. It is clear from the reflection that opened this chapter that the counselor quoted is not only working with a client who is being confronted with a very challenging situation, but she is also having trouble finding a balance herself between professional and personal involvement. When a counselor moves from professional care and empathy to personal emotional involvement, objectivity is lost.

The current chapter addresses the issue of the counselor's loss of professional objectivity and its potential negative effect, not only on the counseling dynamic but also on the well-being of the counselor. After completing the chapter, the reader will be able to complete the following:

a. Describe the unique characteristics of a counseling relationship that challenges the maintenance of professional objectivity.

b. Describe what is meant by identification and countertransference.

c. Explain the potential negative effect of counselor identification or countertransference to both the counseling dynamic and the well-being of the counselor.

The Counseling Relationship: Challenging Objectivity

The counseling relationship is unique among social encounters in that it requires openness and attentiveness, as well as a level of intimacy that is atypical in other professional, nontherapeutic encounters. While the relationship is established and maintained for the benefit of the client, the nature of the relationship is such that it has an effect on the counselor as well.

Counselors approach the counseling relationship with the ethical mandate to maintain a therapeutic level of objectivity and place the client's welfare first (ACA, 2014, A.1.a). Counselor objectivity is a must if clients are to be able to share their stories and find support from a professional who is not only nonjudgmental but can also process the client's story without the distortion of their personal feelings, prejudices, or unresolved issues.

The nature of a counseling relationship, however, is such that it makes it difficult for counselors to maintain professional objectivity and boundaries consistently. While seeking to engage with appropriate professional distancing, the truth is that counselors cannot entirely divorce themselves from their own experiences, values, prejudices, and unfinished business. As Aponte and Winter (1987) noted, "Engaging in therapeutic work with clients is a social context which, for a therapist, jostles his [sic] own personal issues in ways that few other encounters do. The continuous reflection on people's personal struggles ... moves a therapist to seek to resolve his own life issues" (p. 94).

The loss of professional objectivity can not only interfere with a counselor's ability to provide ethical, effective service but also undermine a counselor's well-being. The therapeutic relationship can be one that pulls the counselor toward increased emotional vulnerability (Levine, 2010). This was undoubtedly the case of the domestic abuse counselor with whom we opened the chapter (see Case Illustration 3.1).

CASE ILLUSTRATION 3.1

Beyond Professional Concern: Personal Obsession

If this is how this job goes, I'm not sure I can take it. Everyone at work tells me I'll get used to it, but I don't know if I can. I've only been on the job for 6 weeks, but these people have such horrible stories. How do I leave it at work? How do I just go home at night and act like everything is okay? It's not okay; I just can't shut it down. There has to be more that I can do to help.

I mean, here I am: I have a great apartment, a super boyfriend, great family, food, clothes—everything I could want, and here she is roaming the street trying to find a shelter that has a bed available; otherwise, she's on the street. It is so unfair. I just can't stop thinking about her. I am so worried that something is going to happen to her. She's so vulnerable. Maybe I should let her stay with me until we find something else. What's the big deal? I have the room. What harm would it be?

From Professional to Personal

Working within the parameters of a professional relationship is a definite concern and mandate of all practicing counselors. The ACA Code of Ethics provides clear direction regarding the management and maintenance of boundaries and professional relation-ships (ACA, 2014; Section A6). A similar direction is provided in the ASCA's Ethical Standards for School Counselors that directs school counselors to avoid relationships that might impair their objectivity (ASCA, 2016, A.5.a).

While the ethical directives are clear, and counselors generally seek to adhere to principles of ethical practice, the truth is that the maintenance of professional objectivity and boundaries can be difficult. The erosion of professional boundaries and the introduction of a counselor's personal needs into the counseling relationship can start small and become incrementally problematic. This is true even when the transgression is as grave as the sexual exploitation of a client. Research has found that even sexual transgressions by therapists often unfold as a gradual process, starting with the therapist making simple, personal disclosures and exhibiting very subtle forms of seductive behavior (Somer & Nachmanil, 2005). While little and less severe breaches of professional boundaries may initially go unnoticed, even these are never benign. Practices such as regularly going over scheduled session time, extending appointments outside of the typical workday, offering to provide transportation home, reducing fees beyond that which is standard for the practice, socializing with the client, and frequent and personal texting or e-mailing are all illustrations of minor boundary violations. Each of these variations can become incrementally problematic and start the relationship down a slippery slope, moving a counselor from professional to personal involvement.

Emotional Involvement

Given the level of relational intimacy and the intensity of the issues often presented within counseling, the ability of a counselor to maintain both a sense of empathy and an appropriate emotional distancing is sometimes difficult to achieve. Establishing and maintaining a healthy balance of care and concern with appropriate professional dis-tancing can become a particular challenge for counselors who engage in identification with the client or employ the counseling relationship as a context in which to work out their personal needs and issues.

Identification

Counselor identification is described as the process in which the counselor relates his or her personal experiences with those of the client (Peabody & Gelso, 1982). Depend-ing on the nature of that identification, counselor identification can be a source of increased empathy or a significant precursor to countertransference (Bachrach, 1976; Peabody & Gelso, 1982; Reik, 1964). This dual potential is evident in the experience of the school counselor described in the following case illustration (see Case Illus-tration 3.2).

CASE ILLUSTRATION 3.2

Your Story or Mine?

The client was a 15-year-old high school student who was struggling with the question of how and when to "come out" to her family and friends regarding her sexual orientation. Seeking some support and direction on this very important issue, the student presented her concern to her school counselor. The issue of coming out was one with which this counselor had personal experience, having come out to her family at the age of 14.

While it was clear that this student was comfortable with sharing her information, both with the counselor and her parents, she genuinely sought some assistance with determining the when and how to present her story to her parents. However, in listening to the client's concerns, the counselor felt jettisoned back to her own teen experience with coming out.

For this counselor, coming out to her parents was a very painful experience—one that drove a wedge between herself and her parents for over 10 years. Her parents rejected the notion of their daughter being lesbian and even attempted to take her to a counselor who specialized in sexual reorientation. The conflict between the counselor and her parents went unresolved until she was in her late 20s, living on her own, and in a committed relationship.

In this situation, it was clear that the client and the counselor traveled a similar road to self-acceptance of their sexual orientation and the desire to share that acceptance with her parents. And while such a shared experience may have been useful in the context of this counseling relationship, it appeared that this counselor lost her ability to maintain professional objectivity and projected the totality of her experience onto this client.

Processing the client's story through the lens of her own lived experience resulted in the counselor becoming inappropriately and unnecessarily protective of the student, and she began to subtly direct her to withhold such disclosure until she was in a position to be living on her own.

The usefulness of identification is affected by the degree or intensity of its nature. Identification has been described as occurring along a continuum based on the amount of ego investment and the intensity of the reaction (Racker, 1968; Watkins, 1985). Thus a counselor sharing a common ethnic or cultural background with the client may engage in self-disclosure relating to similar family experiences and practices. This would be the case wherein a counselor and the client share similar stories about the food and rituals they experienced growing up as a member of the same ethnic group. Typically, such identification is of low intensity and low ego involvement. At the other end of the continuum would be the counselor, for example, who as a result of his or her personal history with parental abuse now experiences intense emotional reactions and projection when working with a client sharing a similar abusive experience (see Case Illustration 3.3).

CASE ILLUSTRATION 3.3

Needing a Hug

I am sorry—you can tell me it is illegal or unethical—but she needs a hug, she needs lots of hugs. Those parents have no right having children. All they care about is their work, making money, impressing their friends and all at the expense of this darling, precious little girl.

This comment was made by an elementary school counselor who was expressing her concern for one of her second-grade students. The student, who we will call Amanda, was referred by her teacher, who noted that Amanda "appeared sad a lot of the time and very needy of my (the teacher's) attention."

I am not sure what I can do for her—it is so sad. I worry about her on weekends and whether or not she is just getting dumped on some neighbor or god knows what.

The facts of the situation included the following:

- Amanda's parents, both lawyers, have been working long hours over the past 5 weeks; one or the other parent has had to work on weekends.
- Amanda is very involved with after-school activities, and because of the change in her parents' workload and schedule, she is now taken to her activities by her best friend's parents.
- These past few weeks, only one parent has been able to attend her weekend sporting events (with the parents alternating).
- Amanda shared that she feels sad sometimes in class because her best friend tells stories about her dogs, and Amanda wants a puppy, but her parents told her that they could not get one at this time, and they would get one in the summer when there would be more time available to help train it. Amanda is sad because she "wants it now!"

When presented with the "facts" of the situation, the counselor was quick to respond. "I know you don't get it … but I do. I know exactly how it feels to be unloved or emotionally abandoned by your parents. My parents were so involved in their own lives and their divorce that I felt like a fifth wheel. If it wasn't for my school counselor and my grandmother who made me feel like somebody, I am not sure where I would be."

For identification to occur, the counselor must first perceive a commonality with the client or the client's story and then experience an emotional investment in that facet or theme. It would appear that the more elements with which the counselor can identify and the more intense the emotions associated with those elements, the more potential for the counselor's loss of professional objectivity.

Countertransference

The construct of countertransference has historically been associated with a clinician's unresolved issues and conflicts (Gelso & Hayes, 2007). However, more recent discussions have focused on countertransference as "the entirety of the (therapist's) emotional reactions to the patient within the treatment situation" (Bouchard, Normandin, & Seguin, 1995, p. 719). Given the nature of the counseling relationship and counseling dynamic, it is fair to assume that a counselor will have personal feelings and reactions to his or her clients. As such, it would appear that countertransference feelings would seem inevitable.

Counselor countertransference need not be automatically a bad thing. Ignoring countertransference can, however, be detrimental to the effective, ethical treatment of one's client. It is essential for counselors to differentiate the issues and the emotions that are theirs versus those that are being presented by the client. In the absence of such awareness, it is possible that these unidentified feelings could result in the counselor marginalizing specific topics or allowing them to influence the direction of the treatment. Without a clear recognition of the nature and sources of the countertransference feelings, a counselor's response could be detrimental to him or herself, the client, and the counseling relationship (Singer & Luborsky, 1977).

The directive, therefore, is for counselors to learn to identify countertransference and manage these feelings so that they do not negatively influence their behavior and interfere with the therapeutic process. It is essential for counselors to engage in strategies such as reflecting on sessions, participating in collegial supervision and case conferencing, and journaling about practice decisions to identify if and how their personal histories and experiences may have informed these decisions. Exercise 3.1 invites you to think about those issues that when presented in counseling may elicit your emotional response and thus challenge your professional objectivity.

EXERCISE 3.1

Issues That Challenge Professional Objectivity

Directions: In the following exercise, you will find a listing of topics or issues that can be presented within counseling. You are invited to (1) rate the degree to which you feel the issue would elicit your own emotional response, (2) identify experiences in your own life that may be contributing to these feelings, and (3) identify the degree to which you believe the feelings might challenge your ability to remain professionally objective while working with a client sharing this experience.

Clinical Issue or Topic	Anticipated Emotional Response 5 = very strong 1 = minimal, if any emotional reaction	Personal Experiences Contributing to Your Emotional Response	Potential Impact on Professional Objectivity 5 = significantly interferes with the ability to remain objective to the point of needing to make a client referral 1 = no interference anticipated
The client is a victim of childhood sexual abuse.			
The client is an admitted pedophile.			
The client is an abusive alcoholic.			
The client is diagnosed with borderline personality disorder.			
The client is diagnosed with a narcissistic personality disorder.			
The client is in an abusive marriage.			
The client exhibits a dependent personality.			
The client is a substance abuser.			
The client bullies.			
The client engages in child pornography.			
The client admits to being physically abusive with spouse and children (an issue that "pushes" your emotional button).			

Balancing Engagement and Clinical Detachment

Just as compassion and empathy are essential to provide good quality of care, objectivity is also needed. Counselors need to be empathic but at the same time maintain their professional distance and objectivity. Achieving a balance between empathically caring for a client and keeping a practical level of detachment can be difficult.

The potential for a counseling relationship to become a vehicle for addressing counselor needs is real and has to be defended against by the establishment and maintenance of clear professional boundaries. Inherent in the notion of establishing professional boundaries is that these boundaries serve to create an atmosphere of safety and predictability that facilitate the therapeutic process. Professional boundaries help to articulate the roles of the counselor and the client and the fundamental nature and purpose of their interaction.

Establishing professional boundaries does not imply counselor rigidity or coldness. The establishment of therapeutic boundaries allows for warm, empathic connections while creating a "brake" on a therapist's potential for exerting inappropriate power and engaging in inappropriate roles in response to his or her clients' stories or engaging in personal need satisfaction.

Table 3.1 provides strategies for maintaining professional distance without compromising empathy.

TABLE 3.1   Finding Balance

The following tips will help you maintain professional distance without compromising empathy.

1. Keep work at work
Providing full, competent, and compassionate attention and care for your clients are essential elements of ethical and effective practice. Maintaining your emotional well-being is also key to the provision of ethical and effective practice. A counselor can support her well-being and reinforce personal, emotional boundaries by letting go of client concerns at the end of the workday.

2. Develop practice routines
It is helpful to develop a pattern of professional practice—for example, regarding how you monitor the length of a session, use the time between sessions, and decide on the frequency of scheduling. Significant variation from these routines could serve as an invitation to reflect on the reason for such variation. Are they in service of the client or are they self-serving?

3. Develop practices to facilitate transition
Rituals and practices such as taking a moment to be mindful of your setting before entering your house, changing to leisure clothing, and listening to your favorite music as you travel from work can help to shift your attention from client concern and work when not at the practice.

4. Reduce "work talk"
It may be tempting to share with others the events of your workday; however, doing so not only invites violation of confidentiality but also extends your engagement with work. Identify nonwork issues, topics, and foci to share. Interacting with people outside of the profession is essential for one's well-being. Should professional questions or client issues demand attention, supervision should be sought.

KEYSTONES

- Counselors approach the counseling relationship with the ethical mandate to maintain a therapeutic level of objectivity and to place the client's welfare first.

- The nature of a counseling relationship is such that it makes it difficult for counselors to maintain professional objectivity and professional boundaries consistently.

- The loss of professional objectivity can not only interfere with a counselor's ability to provide ethical, effective service but also undermine a counselor's well-being.

- The erosion of professional boundaries and the introduction of the counselor's needs into the counseling relationship can start small and become incrementally problematic.

- Counselor identification is described as the process in which the counselor relates his or her personal experiences with those of the client (Peabody & Gelso, 1982).

- The construct of countertransference that was historically associated with a clinician's unresolved issues and conflicts is now more broadly viewed as "the entirety of the (therapist's) emotional reactions to the patient within the treatment situation" (Bouchard et al., 1995, p. 719).

- Counselor countertransference need not be automatically a bad thing. Ignoring countertransference can, however, be detrimental to the effective, ethical treatment of one's client.

- Counselors need to be empathic but at the same time maintain their professional distance and objectivity.

- The potential for a counseling relationship to become a vehicle for addressing counselor needs is real and needs to be defended against by the establishment and maintenance of clear professional boundaries.

ADDITIONAL RESOURCES

In Print

Gelso, C. J., & Hayes, J. (2007). *Countertransference and the therapist's inner experience: Perils and possibilities*. Mahwah, NJ: Lawrence Erlbaum Associates, Inc.

Kuttnauer, L. S., & Tuch, R. (Eds.) (2018). *Conundrums and predicaments in psychotherapy*. New York, NY: Routledge.

Pope, K. S., Sonne, J. L., & Greene, B. (2006) *What therapists don't' talk about and why: Understanding taboos that hurt us and our clients*. Washington, DC: American Psychological Association.

Web Based

American Psychological Association. (n.d.) Ethics and complex boundary challenges: What you didn't learn in graduate school [Online course]. Retrieved from https://www.apa.org/education/ce/ccw0039.aspx

Christie, L. (n.d.). Ethics and boundaries in psychotherapy, a 3-hour online continuing education (CE) course. Retrieved from https://www.pdresources.org/blog_data/ethics-boundaries-in-psychotherapy-new-ce-course/

Zur, O. (n.d.). To cross or not to cross: Do boundaries in therapy protect or harm? Retrieved from https://www.zurinstitute.com/boundariesintherapy.html

REFERENCES

American Counseling Association (ACA). (2014). *ACA code of ethics.* Washington, DC: Author.

American School Counselor Association (ASCA). (2016). *ASCA ethical standards for school counselors.* Alexandria, VA: Author.

Aponte, H. J., & Winter, J. E. (1987). The person and practice of the therapist: Treatment and training. *Journal of Psychotherapy and the Family, 3*, 85–111.

Bachrach, H. M. (1976). Empathy: We know what we mean, but what do we measure? *Archives of General Psychiatry, 33*, 35–38.

Bouchard, M., Normandin, L., & Seguin, M. (1995). Countertransference as instrument and obstacle: A comprehensive and descriptive framework. *Psychoanalytic Quarterly, 44*, 717–745.

Gelso, C. J., & Hayes, J. A. (2007). *Countertransference and the therapist's inner experience: Perils and possibilities.* Mahwah, NJ: Erlbaum.

Levine, H. B. (2010). Sexual boundary violations: A psychoanalytic perspective. *British Journal of Psychotherapy, 26*(1), 50–63.

Peabody, S. A., & Gelso, C. J. (1982). Countertransference and empathy: The complex relationship between two divergent concepts in counseling. *Journal of Counseling Psychology, 29*, 240–245.

Racker, H. (1968). *Transference and counter-transference.* New York, NY: International Universities Press, Inc.

Reik, T. (1964). *Listening with the third ear.* New York, NY: Pyramid.

Singer, B. A., & Luborsky, L. (1977). Countertransference: The status of clinical versus quantitative research. In A. Gurman & A. Razin (Eds.), *Effective psychotherapy: Handbook of research* (pp. 433–541). New York, NY: Pergamon Press.

Somer, E., & Nachmanil, I. (2005). Constructions of therapist-client sex: A comparative analysis of retrospective victim report. *Sexual Abuse: A Journal of Research and Treatment, 17*, 47–62.

Watkins, C. E. (1985). Countertransference: Its impact on the counseling situation. *Journal of Counseling and Development, 63*, 356–359.

Compassion Fatigue

> *So here is my client, a 56-year-old woman who was just informed by her husband that he was filing for divorce. She was devastated and in a state of panic. As for me? Nothing. I heard the words, saw the tears—but could not connect with her feelings, nor mine.*
>
> **—Samuel, Counselor in private practice**

Samuel is giving voice to his reduced capacity for empathy. He, at least at this moment, could no longer bear the suffering of his client. Samuel is experiencing compassion fatigue.

Sharing the pain, the anxiety, the dread, and the hopelessness of our clients can deaden our ability to feel and convey compassion. The current chapter will present the "what" and "why" of compassion fatigue. Upon completion of this chapter, you will be able to complete the following:

a. Describe the nature of compassion fatigue as it differs from burnout.

b. Explain the factors contributing to the development of compassion fatigue.

c. Assess your risk and current status in relation to compassion fatigue.

Compassion Fatigue: The Gift and Cost of Empathy

Compassion is a hallmark of counselors, therapists, and health care professionals (Figley, 2002). The value of compassion and empathy to the development and maintenance of an effective counseling relationship can come with a price for the counselor (Figley, 1995). That price is often in the form of the development of compassion fatigue.

Compassion fatigue has been defined as a "state of exhaustion and dysfunction—biologically, psychologically and socially—as a result of prolonged exposure to compassion stress" (Figley, 1995, p. 253). Compassion fatigue takes form in a counselor's loss of ability to provide the same level of compassion and care for a client following repeated exposures to traumatization (Figley, 1998).

With symptoms that often mirror those of post-traumatic disorders (Trippany, Wilcoxon, & Satcher, 2003), compassion fatigue is most often associated with counselors who work with those experiencing trauma (Figley, 2002). Truth be told, compassion fatigue is a challenge for all counselors by the very nature of their deep emotional investment and empathic engagement with their clients.

The qualities that make counselors effective with their clients, qualities such as empathy, compassion, and caring, may also leave them vulnerable to such negative outcomes as compassion fatigue (Figley, 1995; Lawson, Venart, Hazler, & Kottler, 2007). It is our empathic connection with our clients and the often-prolonged exposure to their stories of suffering that fosters the development of compassion fatigue. It is as if our empathy invites us to not only truly understand our clients' stories but also absorb their suffering (Figley, 1995). It is an experience that has a sudden onset, most often coming with little warning.

The Impact

Compassion fatigue appears to be multidimensional in its impact. While described as taking the form of general exhaustion, one often accompanied by feelings of fear and anxiety (Killian, 2008), its potentially detrimental effects are much more widespread. Gentry, Webber, and Baranowsky (2018) identified the impact across physical, behavioral, psychological, and spiritual domains and suggested that it could have a global impact on a health-care provider's identity, self-understanding, and existential well-being.

Physical symptoms have included exhaustion, insomnia, compromised immunity, headaches, stomachaches, sleep disturbance, fatigue, and hypochondria (Mathieu, 2008). *Behavioral symptoms* of compassion fatigue may include increased alcohol intake (and other drugs), anger and irritability, strained personal relationships, absenteeism, avoidance of clients, and impaired clinical decision making (Mathieu, 2008).

Psychological symptoms are perhaps one of the most noticeable impacts on a counselor. Compassion fatigue has been found to result in emotional exhaustion, relational distancing, negative self-image, anxiety, and depression (Dutton & Rubinstein, 1995; Mathieu, 2008). The effect can be disruptive to professional practice in that it can result in a counselor's reduced ability to feel sympathy and empathy while at the same time experiencing resentment, depersonalization, and diminished sense of enjoyment and career satisfaction (Mathieu, 2008). Given the extent of the potential effect of compassion fatigue, it is not surprising that it can diminish a counselor's spiritual awareness and result in a counselor's disinterest in introspection and a decreased ability and interest in discernment (Coetzee & Klopper, 2010).

Given the impacts of compassion fatigue on a counselor, especially the reduction of the counselor's ability to engage empathically with his or her client (Meadors & Lamson, 2008), it is not surprising that a counselor's professional identity and sense of professional calling can be destroyed. This was indeed the case for one high school counselor (see Case Illustration 4.1) whose zest for her profession was suddenly drained and resulted in her doubting her value as a professional and as a person.

CASE ILLUSTRATION 4.1

Why Am I Here?

"I don't know why I am here. I don't know why they keep coming to my office. I have nothing to offer, nothing more to give. Let's face it. I am a fraud. I know the title says 'doctor' and the office is labeled 'counselor,' but it is a sham. I really doubt the value of what I do, what I did … or even the value of being a counselor."

This was the introductory comment made by one high school counselor now turned client being seen by one of the authors (Parsons).

The client shared that she had been a school counselor for 17 years in the same rural district, with the last 5 being spent as the high school counselor. The high school was small, with a student base of 600 students. However, she was the only counselor in the high school and only one of three for the entire district. Her caseload was high, the hours long, and the sense of isolation palpable. However, these were conditions that she knew and had navigated for all of her 17 years in the position. This was the place she found joy and purpose. She was a person who felt called to her profession and, as she noted, saw the opportunity to walk with her students at their time of struggle as "a gift and a blessing."

"I truly love my students. I do. They are so precious, and yet most of them are fighting some horrific conditions. Over 80% of our student body receives some form of federal assistance. This is truly a very poor area. Add to that the reality many of the students I see come from families where alcoholism, drug use, and abuse and domestic violence is rampant. Their stories can break your heart. These kids are not worrying about which college to go to, most are worrying about their safety and survival. I know that sounds dramatic, but it is the truth. Now on top of all of this, over 150 of my students have been displaced and their homes devastated by this storm and its flooding. It's just too much. It's too much for them—and it is too much for me. I feel numb. I am impotent. I am not sure why I am here."

She noted that she had been physically and emotionally spent. "I don't have it together. I can't concentrate. I am having difficulty finding the motivation to leave my bed and go in. And, you know, it is not simply the energy, I mean, why should I? Why would I ever think I could make a difference in their lives. The deck is stacked against them, and there is nothing I can do. Really, tell me, why am I here?"

Are You at Risk? Factors Contributing to the Development of Compassion Fatigue

There are a number of work-related factors and personal characteristics or attributes that have been identified as "risk" factors for the development of compassion fatigue.

Work-Related Factors

Researchers have examined the relationship between compassion fatigue and the organizational contexts in which mental health professionals work (Demerouti, Bakker, Nachreiner, & Schaufeli, 2001; Lent & Schwartz, 2012). Counselors who work in the area of crises and trauma or those working with clients reporting abuse appear to have an increased susceptibility to compassion fatigue (Pearlman & Saakvitne, 1995). Other work-related factors such as heavy caseloads, inordinately long hours, working in professional isolation, and limited collegial support also appear to place a counselor at greater risk of experiencing compassion fatigue (Collins & Long, 2003a; Craig & Sprang, 2010; Flannelly, Roberts, & Weaver, 2005). In Exercise 4.1, we invite you to investigate the factors that may contribute to compassion fatigue in the setting in which you plan to work (see Exercise 4.1).

EXERCISE 4.1

Work-Related Factors

Directions: Interview a counselor in the setting in which you are planning to work. Ask the following questions and then process your responses with a supervisor or professional colleague.
Questions for Interview:

1. What factors make it more difficult to do your job effectively?

2. What types of support do you have or wish that you had?

3. What tasks take time away from your primary role as a counselor, and how does this impact your job?

4. What do you think is most difficult about your job in this setting?

5. How long have you been a counselor? How long have you been in this setting?

Questions for Processing:

1. Did the interviewee's answers surprise you? Why/why not?

2. Do the supports appear to be sufficient?

3. Do you think the counselor could use more support? Elaborate on your answer.

4. What do you think is most helpful for the counselor to deal with compassion fatigue in this setting?

5. What do you anticipate needing/doing in this setting to deal with compassion fatigue?

Personal Characteristics

While it appears that work or contextual factors can contribute to a counselor's risk of developing compassion fatigue, these alone do not appear to account fully for a counselor's vulnerability (Linley & Joseph, 2007).

Research (e.g., Meadors & Lamson, 2008) suggests that counselors who tend to be overly conscientious, who are unable to leave work at work, and who employ high standards and expectations appear to be at greater risk for compassion fatigue. Further, when high levels of personal stress or trauma exist, especially when experienced in the absence of social support, the risk potential for a counselor's experience of compassion fatigue is increased (Meadors & Lamson, 2008). Perhaps the one characteristic that places a counselor most at risk for compassion fatigue is the ability of a counselor to engage empathically with a client. While such a capability is essential to effective counseling, it also invites the counselor to have a vicarious experience with the client's pain. As suggested by Stebnicki (2000), compassion fatigue is the outgrowth of the "empathic connection [human service professionals] maintain with their clients" (p. 23). Exercise 4.2 is an opportunity to reflect on your personal experience(s) with compassion fatigue.

EXERCISE 4.2

A Reflection on Your Personal Experiences With Compassion Fatigue

Directions: Think of a time when you struggled with being sympathetic or empathic with another person (it could be a family member, a neighbor, a coworker, or a case about a person on the evening news). What was the person's story? What would you say precipitated your inability to sympathize or empathize? What would be your reaction to that same situation or story if you encountered it today? Do you feel any different about it? Is your reaction the same or different? If it is the same, how might you be able to work on this?

The characteristics noted may actively contribute to a counselor's vulnerability to the development of compassion fatigue. It would appear that this vulnerability is also increased when specific self-care practices (Kraus, 2005; Venart, Vassos, & Pritcher-Heft, 2007), mindfulness attitudes and practices (Valenta & Marotta, 2005; Vilardaga et al. 2011), and engagement in sustaining relationships (Stamm, 2002) are absent from a counselor's life. These factors, along with other stress-reduction activities associated with physical health, leisure activities, spiritual-oriented activities (Wallace, Lee & Lee, 2010), and supervision, can serve as a buffer for the development of compassion fatigue, and their absence increases the vulnerability and risk of the counselor.

Detection: Knowing the Symptoms

No one is immune from the possibility of experiencing compassion fatigue. Counselors who do not recognize and/or cope with the symptoms of compassion fatigue sometimes are challenged in their ability to provide effective services and maintain positive personal and professional relationships (Collins & Long, 2003b).

While there are steps that can be taken to reduce the possibility of experiencing compassion fatigue or intervening when needed (Chapters 8, 9, and 10), the truth is that a step that all counselors should employ is to monitor their levels of compassion satisfaction and fatigue regularly. One approach is to take time to reflect on those symptoms most often indicative of compassion fatigue, informally assessing the degree to which the counselor might be experiencing them at any one point. A list of symptoms associated with compassion fatigue (Gentry, 2002) is presented in Exercise 4.3. It is suggested that counselors use such a listing to guide regular self-monitoring of their state of well-being.

EXERCISE 4.3

Monitoring Symptoms Associated With Compassion Fatigue

Directions: In the following exercise, you will find a comprehensive listing of symptoms associated with compassion fatigue. It is suggested that you review the list, noting those symptoms that you have experienced in the past 30 days. This informal listing can be used to monitor your current state of well-being and the possibility of experiencing compassion fatigue.

Intrusive Symptoms

_____ ▪ Thoughts and images associated with the client's traumatic experiences

_____ ▪ Obsessive and compulsive desires to help certain clients

_____ ▪ Client/work issues encroaching on personal time

_____ ▪ Inability to "let go" of work-related matters

_____ ▪ Perception of survivors as fragile and needing the assistance of a caregiver ("savior")

_____ ▪ Thoughts and feelings of inadequacy as a caregiver

_____ ▪ Sense of entitlement or specialness

_____ ▪ Perception of the world regarding victims and perpetrators

_____ ▪ Personal activities interrupted by work-related issues

Avoidance Symptoms

_____   ▪ Silencing response (avoiding hearing/witnessing client's
traumatic material)

_____   ▪ Loss of enjoyment in activities/cessation of self-care activities

_____   ▪ Loss of energy

_____   ▪ Loss of hope/sense of dread working with certain clients

_____   ▪ Loss of a sense of competence/potency

_____   ▪ Isolation

_____   ▪ Secretive self-medication/addiction (alcohol, drugs, work, sex,
food, spending, etc.)

_____   ▪ Relational dysfunction

Arousal Symptoms

_____   ▪ Increased anxiety

_____   ▪ Impulsivity/reactivity

_____   ▪ Increased perception of demand/threat (in both job
and environment)

_____   ▪ Increased frustration/anger

_____   ▪ Sleep disturbance

_____   ▪ Difficulty concentrating

_____   ▪ Change in weight/appetite

_____   ▪ Somatic symptoms

Symptoms Source: Gentry, J. E. (2002). Compassion fatigue: A crucible of transformation. *Journal of Trauma Practice, 1*(3/4), 36–71. Retrieved from http://marchandchris.tripod.com/PDF/ACrucibleofTransformation.pdf

In addition to such an informal assessment and self-monitoring, there are a number of standardized instruments that have been demonstrated to be useful in the assessment of compassion fatigue. It should be noted, however, that the assessment of compassion fatigue is difficult given the variety of definitions and taxonomies employed (Naijar et al., 2009) and the scoring guidelines are often quite conservative (Bride et al., 2007). Thus these measures should not be used as a diagnostic test. They are intended to serve as screening tools to aid in the identification of compassion fatigue (Stamm, 2010).

Measures currently employed to assess compassion fatigue include the Compassion Fatigue Self-Test (CFST) (Figley & Stamm, 1996), the Compassion Fatigue Scale (CFS-R) (Adams et al., 2008), and, perhaps one of the most popular assessment instruments, the Professional Quality of Life Scale (ProQOL) (Stamm, 2012).

The ProQOL 5 Self-Score measure is in its fifth iteration. The ProQOL is offered in 25 languages and can be directly accessed at https://proqol.org/ProQol_Test.html. The ProQOL has subscales that assess compassion satisfaction, fatigue, and burnout. The scales for compassion satisfaction and fatigue are listed in Figure 4.1, and counselors would do well to use the scale to monitor their current levels of compassion satisfaction and fatigue regularly.

FIGURE 4.1 ProQOL Compassion Satisfaction Subscale

COMPASSION SATISFACTION AND COMPASSION FATIGUE (PROQOL) VERSION 5 (2009)

When you *[help]* people you have direct contact with their lives. As you may have found, your compassion for those you *[help]* can affect you in positive and negative ways. Below are some questions about your experiences, both positive and negative, as a *[helper]*. Consider each of the following questions about you and your current work situation. Select the number that honestly reflects how frequently you experienced these things in the *last 30 days*.

1 = Never	**2 = Rarely**	**3 = Sometimes**	**4 = Often**	**5 = Very Often**

_____ 1. I am happy.

_____ 2. I am preoccupied with more than one person I *[help]*.

_____ 3. I get satisfaction from being able to *[help]* people.

_____ 4. I feel connected to others.

_____ 5. I jump or am startled by unexpected sounds.

_____ 6. I feel invigorated after working with those I *[help]*.

_____ 7. I find it difficult to separate my personal life from my life as a *[helper]*.

_____ 8. I am not as productive at work because I am losing sleep over the traumatic experiences of a person I help.

_____ 9. I think that I might have been affected by the traumatic stress of those I *[help]*.

_____ 10. I feel trapped by my job as a *[helper]*.

_____ 11. Because of my *[helping]*, I have felt "on edge" about various things.

_____ 12. I like my work as a *[helper]*.

_____ 13. I feel depressed because of the traumatic experiences of the people I *[help]*.

_____ 14. I feel as though I am experiencing the trauma of someone I have *[helped]*.

_____ 15. I have beliefs that sustain me.

_____ 16. I am pleased with how I am able to keep up with *[helping]* techniques and protocols.

_____ 17. I am the person I always wanted to be.

_____ 18. My work makes me feel satisfied.

_____ 19. I feel worn out because of my work as a *[helper]*.

_____ 20. I have happy thoughts and feelings about those I *[help]* *and* how I could help them.

_____ 21. I feel overwhelmed because my case [work] load seems endless.

_____ 22. I believe I can make a difference through my work.

_____ 23. I avoid certain activities or situations because they remind me of the frightening experiences of the people I *[help]*.

_____ 24. I am proud of what I can do to *[help]*.

_____ 25. As a result of my *[helping]*, I have intrusive, frightening thoughts.

_____ 26. I feel "bogged down" by the system.

_____ 27. I have thoughts that I am a "success" as a *[helper]*.

_____ 28. I can't recall important parts of my work with trauma victims.

_____ 29. I am a very caring person.

_____ 30. I am happy that I chose to do this work

Copy your rating on each of these questions on to this table and add them up. Check your score against the interpretation provided.

3.			
6.	**The sum of my Compassion Satisfaction questions is**	**So My Score Equals**	**And my Compassion Satisfaction level is**
12.			
16.	22 or less	43 or less	Low
18.	Between 23 and 41	Around 50	Average
20.	42 or more	57 or more	High
22.			
24.			
27.			
TOTAL			

Compassion Satisfaction

Compassion satisfaction is about the pleasure you derive from being able to do your work well.

The average score is 50 (SD 10; alpha scale reliability .88). About 25% of people score higher than 57, and about 25% of people score below 43. If you are in the higher range, you probably derive a good deal of professional satisfaction from your position. If your scores are below 40, you may either find problems with your job, or there may be some other reason—for example, you might derive your satisfaction from activities other than your job.

Copy your rating on each of these questions on to this table and add them up. Check your score against the interpretation provided.

3.			
6.	**The sum of my Compassion Satisfaction questions is**	**So My Score Equals**	**And my Compassion Satisfaction level is**
12.			
16.	22 or less	43 or less	Low
18.	Between 23 and 41	Around 50	Average
20.	42 or more	57 or more	High
22.			
24.			
27.			
TOTAL			

Compassion Satisfaction

Compassion satisfaction is about the pleasure you derive from being able to do your work well. The average score is 50 (SD 10; alpha scale reliability .88). About 25% of people score higher than 57, and about 25% of people score below 43. If you are in the higher range, you probably derive a good deal of professional satisfaction from your position. If your scores are below 40, you may either find problems with your job, or there may be some other reason—for example, you might derive your satisfaction from activities other than your job.

KEYSTONES

- Compassion fatigue has been defined as a "state of exhaustion and dysfunction—biologically, psychologically and socially—as a result of prolonged exposure to compassion stress" (Figley, 1995, p. 253).

- Compassion fatigue appears to be multidimensional. Symptoms can appear across physical, behavioral, psychological, and spiritual domains and result in detriment to the counselor's professional identity and existential well-being.

- Counselors who work in the area of crises and trauma or those working with clients reporting abuse appear to have an increased susceptibility to compassion fatigue (Pearlman & Saakvitne, 1995).

- Heavy caseloads, inordinately long hours, working in professional isolation, and limited collegial support also appear to place a counselor at greater risk of experiencing compassion fatigue (Collins & Long, 2003a; Craig & Sprang, 2010; Flannelly et al., 2005).

- Counselors who tend to be overly conscientious, who are unable to leave work at work, and who employ high standards and expectations appear to be at greater risk for compassion fatigue.

- Counselors experiencing high levels of personal stress or trauma, especially when in the absence of social support, have an elevated risk of compassion fatigue (Meadors & Lamson, 2008).

- Measures currently employed to assess compassion fatigue include the CFST (Figley & Stamm, 1996), CFS-R (Adams et al., 2008), and, perhaps one of the most popular assessment instruments, the ProQOL (Stamm, 2012).

ADDITIONAL RESOURCES

In Print

Kottler, J. A. (2012). *The therapist's workbook: Self-assessment, self-care and self-improvement exercises for mental health professionals* (2nd ed.). Hoboken, NJ: John Wiley & Sons.

McCann, I. L., & Pearlman, L. A. (1990). *Psychological trauma and the adult survivor: Theory, therapy, and transformation.* New York, NY: Brunner/Mazel.

Racanelli, Christine. (2005). "Is it burnout and/or compassion fatigue? How to identify, differentiate, prevent and intervene." New York University School of Social Work. http://docplayer.net/96724629-National-child-welfare-resource-center-for-adoption-at-spaulding-for-children.html

Stebnicki, M. A. (2008). *Empathy fatigue: Healing the mind, body, and spirit of professional counselors.* New York, NY: Springer.

Web Based

ACA's Taskforce on Counselor Wellness and Impairment: http://www.counseling. org/wellness_taskforce/index.htm

Compassion Fatigue Self-Test: http://www.ptsdsupport.net/compassion_fatugue-selftest.html

Professional Quality of Life Inventory (ProQOL), Fifth Edition: www.proqol.org

REFERENCES

Adams, R. E., Boscarino, J. A., & Figley, C. R. (2008). The compassion fatigue scale: Its use with social workers following urban disaster. *Research on Social Work Practice*, *18*(3), 238–250.

Bride, E., Radey, M., & Figley, C. R. (2007). Measuring compassion fatigue. *Clinical Social Work Journal*, *35*, 155–163.

Collins, S., & Long, A. (2003a). Working with the psychological effects of trauma: Consequences for mental health-care workers: A literature review. *Journal of Psychiatric and Mental Health, Nursing*, *10*, 417–424.

Collins, S. & Long A. (2003b). Too tired to care? The psychological effects of working with trauma. *Journal of Psychiatric and Mental Health Nursing*, *10*, 17–27.

Coetzee, S., & Klopper, H. (2010). Compassion fatigue within nursing practice: A concept analysis. *Nursing Health Science*, *12*, 235–243.

Craig, C., & Sprang, G. (2010). Compassion satisfaction, compassion fatigue, and burnout in a national sample of trauma treatment therapists. *Anxiety, Stress & Coping*, *23*, 319–339.

Demerouti, E., Bakker, A. B., Nachreiner, F., & Schaufeli, W. B. (2001). The job demands resources model of burnout. *Journal of Applied Psychology*, *86*, 499–512.

Dutton, M. A., & Rubinstein, F. L. (1995). Working with people with PTSD: Research implications. In C. R. Figley (Ed.), *Compassion fatigue: Secondary traumatic stress disorder in helpers* (pp. 82–100). New York, NY: Brunner/Mazel.

Figley, C. R. (1995). Compassion fatigue as secondary traumatic stress disorder: An overview. *Compassion fatigue: Coping with secondary traumatic stress disorder in those who treat the traumatized*. New York, NY: Brunner/Mazel.

Figley C. R. (1998). *Burnout in families: The systemic costs of caring*. Boca Raton, FL: CRC Press.

Figley, C. R. (2002). *Treating compassion fatigue*. New York, NY: Brunner/Mazel.

Figley, C. R., & Stamm, B. H. (1996). Psychometric review of compassion fatigue self-test. In B. H. Stamm (Ed.), *Measurement of stress, trauma and adaptation*. Lutherville, MD: Sidran Press.

Flannelly, K., Roberts, S., & Weaver, A. (2005). Correlates of compassion fatigue and burnout in chaplains and other clergy who responded to September 11th attacks in New York City. *Journal of Pastoral Care and Counseling*, *58*, 231–234.

Gentry, J. E., Baranowsky, A. B., & Dunnin, K. (2002). The accelerated recovery program (ARP) for compassion fatigue. In C. R. Figley (Ed.), *Treating compassion fatigue* (pp. 123–138). New York, NY: Brunner-Routledge.

Gentry, J. E., Webber, J. M., & Baranowsky, A. B (2018). Compassion fatigue: Our Achilles heel. In J. M. Webber & J. B. Mascari (Eds.), *Disaster mental health counseling: A guide to preparing and responding* (4th ed., pp. 79–92). Alexandria, VA: American Counseling Association Foundation.

Kassam-Adams, N. (1999). The risk of treating sexual trauma: Sex and secondary trauma in psychotherapists. In H. B. Stamm (Ed.), *Secondary traumatic stress: Self-care issues for clinicians, researchers and educators* (2nd ed., pp. 37–48). Lutherville, MD: Sidran Press.

Killian, K. D. (2008). Helping till it hurts? A multimethod study of compassion fatigue, burnout, and self-care in clinicians working with trauma survivors. *Traumatology, 14*, 32–44.

Kraus, V. I. (2005). Relationship between self-care and compassion satisfaction, compassion fatigue, and burnout among mental health professionals working with adolescent sex offenders. *Counseling and Clinical Psychology Journal, 2*, 81–88.

Lawson, G., & Myers, J. E. (2011). Wellness, professional quality of life, and career-sustaining behaviors: What keeps us well? *Journal of Counseling & Development, 89*, 163–171.

Lawson, G., Venart, E., Hazler, R. J., & Kottler, J. A. (2007). Toward a culture of counselor wellness. *Journal of Humanistic Counseling, Education and Development, 46*, 5–19.

Lent, J., & Schwartz, R. (2012). The impact of work setting, demographic characteristics, and personality factors related to burnout among professional counselors. *Journal of Mental Health Counseling, 34*, 355–372.

Linley, P. A., & Joseph, S. (2007). Therapy work and therapists' positive and negative well-being. *Journal of Social and Clinical Psychology, 26*, 385–403.

Mathieu, F. (2008). *The compassion fatigue workbook.* Retrieved from www.compassionfatigue.ca

Meadors, P., & Lamson, A. (2008). Compassion fatigue and secondary traumatization: Provider self care on the intensive care units for children. *Journal of Pediatric Health, 22*(1), 24–34.

Naijar, N., Davis, L.W., Beck-Coon, K., & Carney Doebbeling, C. (2009). Compassion fatigue: A review of the research to date and relevance to cancer-care providers. *Journal of Health Psychology, 14*(2), 267–277.

Pearlman, L. A., & Saakvitne, K. W. (1995). Treating therapists with vicarious traumatization and secondary traumatic stress disorders. In C. R. Figley (Ed.), *Compassion fatigue: Coping with secondary traumatic stress disorder in those who treat the traumatized* (pp. 150–177). New York, NY: Brunner Mazel.

Stamm, B. H. (2002). Measuring compassion satisfaction as well as fatigue: Developmental history of the compassion satisfaction and fatigue test. In C. R. Figley (Ed.), *Treating compassion fatigue* (pp. 107–119). New York, NY: Brunner-Routledge.

Stamm, R. H. (2010). *The concise ProQOL manual* (2nd ed.). Pocatello, ID: ProQOL.org

Stamm, B. H. (2012). The professional quality of life scale (ProQOL 5). Retrieved from http://proqol.org/ProQol_Test.html

Stebnicki, M. A. (2000). Stress and grief reactions among rehabilitation professionals: Dealing effectively with empathy fatigue. *Journal of Rehabilitation, 66*, 23–29.

Trippany, R. L., Wilcoxon, S. A., & Satcher, J. F. (2003). Factors influencing vicarious trauma for therapists of survivors of sexual victimization. *Journal of Trauma Practice, 2*, 47–60.

Valenta, V., & Marotta, A. (2005). The impact of yoga on the professional and personal life of the psychotherapist. *Contemporary Family Therapy, 16*, 99–111.

Venart, E., Vassos, S., & Pritcher-Heft, H. (2007). What individual counselors can do to sustain wellness. *The Journal of Humanistic Counseling, Education and Development, 46*, 50–65.

Vilardaga, R., Luoma, J. B., Hayes, S. C., Pistorello, J., Levin, M. E., Hildebrandt, M. J., & Bond, F. (2011). Burnout among the addiction counseling workforce: The differential roles of mindfulness and values-based processes and work-site factors. *Journal of Substance Abuse Treatment, 40*, 323–335.

Wallace, S., Lee, J., & Lee, S. M. (2010). Job stress, coping strategies, and burnout among abuse specific counselors. *Journal of Employment Counseling, 47*, 111–122.

5

Burnout

I came this close to simply walking away; it all seemed so hopeless, and I was exhausted.

—Elisha, Middle School Counselor

The comment shared by middle school counselor Elisha was a prefacing comment to a very personal description of what came close to the end of her professional career. Elisha shared that she was in her third year as a school counselor and had found the school year to be challenging starting from day one. She felt as if she had been "running out of energy" and had no real "interest in engaging with the students, teachers, or parents." While the entire year was a struggle, Elisha noted that as it was late April, following an extended period of what seemed like "crises after crises," she had decided to take a walk around the track to try to clear her head. In the process of walking, she found herself stuck in thoughts about her inadequacy as a counselor; she realized that she no longer felt the excitement about seeing the students and concluded that it was all too hopeless for what she now evaluated as her own incompetence. As Elisha walked, she found herself spontaneously crying and feeling as if her legs were too heavy to continue; she began to think about merely walking to her car and leaving, to never return.

Elisha's feelings of physical, psychological, and emotional exhaustion were clear indications that she was in the grips of professional burnout. This experience is not limited to those serving in the role of school counselors. Counselors practicing in varied professional settings have shared similar experiences and with a wide variety of clients (Deighton, Gurris, & Traue, 2007; Whealin et al., 2007). The very nature of the role of counselor and the stress associated with that role can, if untreated, result in burnout (Whealin et al., 2007).

It is the experience of burnout, with its negative and destructive impact on one's personal and professional life, that is the focus of the current chapter. Upon completion of this chapter, you will be able to complete the following:

a. Describe the nature of burnout.

b. Explain the factors contributing to the development of burnout.

c. Describe steps to be taken to prevent and, when it is necessary, intervene with burnout.

d. Develop an initial personal self-care plan.

Our Professional Mandate

While it would be comforting to assume that the professional counselor, with all her or his training, is immune to the experience of professional burnout, such is not the case. Counseling is not a profession where one can merely "show up" or "call in." Counselors, be they working in schools, hospitals, agencies, or private practice, are called to walk with their clients as they navigate a wide range of personal challenges. Counseling is a profession and process that demands counselors make themselves available to the emotional experiences of their clients.

The fact that counselors experience stress in the workplace should not be surprising. The stress encountered by counselors stems from both the nature of the work and the role expectations of the profession (Evans & Villavisanis, 1997). For example, counselors working within the school setting are often assigned noncounselor duties. Such assignments have been found to be predictive of burnout for school counselors (Bardhoshi, Schweinle & Duncan, 2014; McCarthy, Van Horn Kerne, Calfa, Lambert, & Guzman, 2010). Caring for others presents many physical, mental, and emotional challenges (Osborn, 2004). High work demands, insufficient resources, role ambiguity, and role conflict are commonplace in the life of the professional counselor (Osborn, 2004).

In his book *On Being a Therapist* (1989), Jeffrey Kottler provides a poignant description of life as a mental health provider. "The therapist enters the relationship with clarity, openness, and serenity and comes fully prepared to encounter a soul in torment" (Kottler, 1989, p. 3). He continues,

> To take on a client, any client, is to make tremendous commitment ... it will have moments of special closeness and times of great hardship. The client will, at times, worship the counselor, scorn the counselor, abuse the counselor, and even play with the counselor. Through it all, regardless of what is going on in the counselor's own life—sickness, births, deaths, joys, disappointment—she must be there for the client, always waiting. (1989, p. 8)

Counselors are more than aware of the gift that is their profession. Being a counselor is a gift, but it is a gift that can come with a cost. Counselors engage in emotionally demanding work and do so often alone, in isolation, enveloped in confidentiality. Walking with those experiencing emotional upset can take a toll on the counselor (O'Brien, 2011; Lee et al., 2007). The stress experienced as a counselor can affect not only the counselor's personal life but also interfere with the professional functioning toward their clients (Skosnik, Chatterton, & Swisher, 2000). Given the real potential of doing harm to one's clients as a result of professional burnout, recognizing and addressing the potential of burnout is more than a good idea; it is an ethical mandate.

The need to monitor a counselor's emotional and physical health, as well as practice wellness, is clearly stated in our codes of ethics. The ACA directs its members to "monitor themselves for signs of impairment of their own physical, mental, or emotional problems and refrain from offering or providing professional services when impaired. They seek assistance for problems that reach the level of professional impairment, and, if necessary, they limit, suspend, or terminate their professional responsibilities until it is determined that they may safely resume their work (ACA, 2014, C.2.g.).

A similar directive is given in the Ethical Standards of the ASCA (2016) to its members noting that school counselors: "Monitor their emotional and physical health and practice wellness to ensure optimal professional effectiveness. School counselors seek physical or mental health support when needed to ensure professional competence" (ASCA, 2016, B.3.f).

Also, for those engaged as mental health counselors, the American Mental Health Counselors Association (AMHCA) is clear in directing its members to "recognize that their effectiveness is dependent on their own mental and physical health. Should their involvement in any activity, or any mental, emotional, or physical health problem, compromise sound professional judgment and competency, they seek capable professional assistance to determine whether to limit, suspend, or terminate services to their clients" (AMHCA 2015, C.1.h.).

Burnout: Insidious and Multidimensional

In reviewing the experience of the school counselor Elisha, with whom we opened this chapter, one might conclude that burnout is an experience that has an abrupt onset. This is not the case. Burnout, by nature an insidious experience, has no clear beginning or ending, but slowly increases its damage over time. Burnout appears to be the cumulative effect of witnessing and engaging with humans who are suffering (O'Brien, 2011; Webb, 2011).

In addition to taking hold over an extended period, burnout shows itself across many modalities. Burnout is genuinely multidimensional in its impact. Maslach (1982) identified three distinct elements of burnout. The first element is depersonalization, which Maslach (1982) defined as "viewing other people through rust-colored glasses, developing a poor opinion of them, expecting the worst from them, and even actively disliking them" (p. 4). A second element, according to Maslach, is the experience of emotional exhaustion, where a counselor simply feels as if there is nothing left to give. The final element described by Maslach was that with burnout, there is a "tendency to evaluate oneself negatively, particularly concerning one's work with clients" (Maslach, Jackson, & Leiter 1996, p. 4). Case Illustration 5.1 highlights the effect of burnout on one mental health counselor.

Jason: A Case of Burnout

Jason is a mental health counselor providing therapeutic services to an urban, adolescent population. He has served as a mentor for many of his colleagues and has provided numerous presentations at local and state professional conferences. By all accounts, Jason is a model of what a counselor should be.

The persona exhibited would lead those with whom he works to believe that Jason has "it all together." Sadly, that external presentation belies the struggle he has been feeling over the past four months. What started out as physical fatigue, fatigue that he attributed to getting older and taking on increasing work responsibilities, began to evolve into a state of weariness at work and a real doubting of the value of his service.

As he described his evolving experience to a therapist, he noted that he had become increasingly numb at work, feeling engulfed in a state of lethargy. He even contacted his human resources department to inquire about his benefits upon retirement. Jason was finding that the career that he loved was now becoming a job. No longer did he experience the joy, the excitement, the "gift" of being a counselor. As he described it, "The excitement, the joy, the daily sense of wonder that I had for the past 12 years has dimmed. I find myself closing the door, finding excuses for why I can't engage with my colleagues, such as being too busy with paperwork, things like that. I have even found myself hoping that clients would cancel appointments. However, even more than this feeling of emptiness, I am concerned that my frustration tolerance has gone out the window."

The incident that served as the stimulus for Jason seeking therapeutic support occurred while interacting with a teen with particular cognitive challenges. Jason explained one specific interaction that seemed to upset him and challenge his view of his own professionalism.

> Jules is one of my clients, and we have been working on his social anxiety and behavioral difficulties at school. He came to the office quite upset about having misplaced his assignment book. Now, Jules has cognitive difficulties and a lot of challenges with keeping his focus and attention. We have been working for weeks on developing his use of an assignment book. Jason had been doing well, and he was quite proud of himself.

> Well, as he sat with me it seemed as if we were starting from the beginning. He began repeating himself and was having difficulty focusing. Now, this was nothing new. What surprised me was that I was extremely frustrated and found myself raising my voice. This is not me. It is not what I would do, but here I was doing it. At one point, I found myself saying, "What is wrong with you that you can't keep a stupid book?" As soon the words left my mouth, I wish I could have sucked them back in. I felt sick to my stomach, and Jules became quite upset. I immediately apologized and made an excuse that I wasn't feeling well, and, thank God, Jules accepted my explanation and apology. However, I was appalled. I damn near went to my supervisor to tell him I quit!

TABLE 5.1 The Multidimensional Nature of Burnout

Domain	Symptoms
Physical	Low energy, chronic fatigue and exhaustion, sleep difficulties, headaches, and gastrointestinal disturbances
Emotional	Boredom, moodiness, annoyance, and frustration to feelings of depression, anxiety, helplessness, and hopelessness (Lambie, 2002; Maslach et al., 2001)
Cognitive	Loss of a sense of accomplishment, increased cynicism, and negative attitudes to depersonalization (Maslach & Jackson, 1986; Maslach et al., 2001)
Social/Interpersonal	Increase in social withdrawal, dehumanizing attitude toward clients, elevated aggression, defensiveness, substance abuse and absenteeism (Lambie, 2002)
Spirituality/Value	Loss of faith, loss of meaning and purpose, feelings of alienation and estrangement, despair, and changes in values, religious beliefs, and religious affiliation (Maslach et al., 2001)

While burnout can negatively affect one's emotional state, it can also negatively affect one's cognitive ability and physical energy and even result in spiritual exhaustion (Gladding, 2011; Maslach, Schaufeli, & Leiter, 2001). The breadth of impact can be seen in Table 5.1.

What becomes evident from a brief review of the symptom listing in Table 5.1 is that burnout not only has a negative effect on the counselor but also that it can interfere with the quality of care a counselor can provide his clients.

Factors Contributing to Burnout

There is no one single cause of burnout; however, a number of factors have been found to contribute to the occurrence of burnout. Factors such as long hours, heavy caseloads, and isolation within the work setting, along with unrealistic role expectations, have all been reported to contribute to the development of burnout (Bardhoshi et al., 2014; Evans & Villavisanis, 1997; McCarthy et al., 2010; Schaufeli, 2003). Given these elements, it should not be a surprise that counselors are vulnerable to experiencing burnout. The stresses encountered by counselors stem from both the nature of the work and the role expectations of the profession (Evans & Villavisanis, 1997). Caring for others presents many physical, mental, and emotional challenges (Osborn, 2004).

Table 5.2 provides a listing of factors contributing to the development of burnout.

Beyond the factors listed in Table 5.2 and perhaps more significantly is the fact that the very nature of what counselors do invites them into the upset and pain of their clients. Core to effective counseling is the counselor's ability to experience and convey empathy. This empathy, as noted by Larson (1993), is "a double-edged sword; it is simultaneously your greatest asset and a point of real vulnerability" (p. 30). Experiencing the depth of feeling expressed by a client in crisis demands a lot from the counselor, and it can take its toll. The work of counselors is genuinely emotionally draining, making them vulnerable to burnout (Bakker, Van der Zee, Lewig, & Dollard, 2006; Skovholt, 2001.)

TABLE 5.2 Factors Contributing to Burnout

1. Unrealistic expectations: Counselors who approach their work with unrealistic expectations position themselves for burnout. Given the large caseloads and the multiple duties often assigned, it is vital that counselors maintain high hopes while at the same time setting realistic expectations. Awareness of the limits of counseling as a process and their power and influence is essential to protect against burnout.

2. Overpersonalization: Taking total responsibility for the client's progress and the outcome of counseling places the counselor at risk of burnout. While bringing expertise to the process, successful outcomes are a result of multiple member engagements, including the counselor, client, and, often, others, such as family members.

3. Loss of objectivity: Counselors care deeply for their clients and should. It is essential, however, that the nature of that care and concern is contained within professional boundaries. For counselors who closely identify with the client or the client's problem, they not only risk the loss of professional objectivity but also the experience of burnout.

4. Task overload: Exhaustion as a significant facet of burnout is easily nurtured by taking on more than can be done given the realities of time and energy. For too many counselors, there are just too many tasks assigned, and the result is physical and psychological exhaustion.

5. Isolation and lack of support: Working behind closed doors and being the keeper of "secrets" and confidential information can result in a counselor's experience of isolation and going it alone. Without collegial dialogue, supervision, and even personal therapy, the counselor raises the risk of burnout.

Adapted from Parsons, R. & Zhang, N. (2013). *Becoming a skilled helper*. Thousand Oaks, CA: Sage Publications, Inc.

A Journey Toward Burnout

As noted previously, burnout is a condition that takes shape over time (Hamann & Gordon, 2000). It is not unusual for those in the grips of burnout to experience sleeplessness, headaches, irritability, emotional and physical exhaustion, and even aggressive behavior (McMullen & Krantz, 1988).

While there is no stepwise set of stages to indicate the unfolding of burnout, for many, the experience begins as a state of emotional exhaustion. This often takes form in a general loss of caring or real interest in their work. For some, this disinterest gives way to negative feelings and attitudes toward clients.

A counselor's complaints about a student who is a "frequent flyer" or client who is "needy," even to the point of blaming the client for the limited progress and outcome is symptomatic of such an attitudinal shift. It is not unusual to find a counselor who is experiencing burnout to objectify the client, seeing him or her as a label or a task rather than a person who is struggling. This may be exhibited in comments such as, "Oh, I have to see my 'whiner' or 'borderline' or 'couple from hell' today." Such labeling not only dehumanizes the client but also provides clear evidence of detachment from the counseling relationship (Maslach et al., 2001). By disengaging from the intensity of an "I-thou" relationship, the counselor can experience a disengagement from empathic attachment and the resulting emotional drain that it elicits can be reduced (Skovholt, 2001).

For those who felt a calling to work in such a responsible and sensitive role like counseling, the use of such "labeling" and the resulting dehumanizing of the client is antithetical to not only the role and function of a counselor but also to all that they valued.

As burnout continues to develop and the counselor experiences difficulty in sustaining an empathic connection, she may exhibit a distancing from the client and a general discouragement and apathy (Fothergill, Edwards, & Burnard, 2004). These conditions make it hard for her to fulfill her professional duties and positions that counselor to feel hopeless about her work (Lee, Chos, Kissinger, & Ogle, 2010; Morse, Salyers, Rollins, Monroe-DeVita, & Pfahler, 2012).

Responding to the Threat of Burnout

Counselors, regardless of the setting or population with whom they work, are at risk for burnout. Given this reality, it is essential that all counselors engage in actions that not only intervene at times of struggle but can also serve a preventive value by increasing the counselor's state of resiliency and emotional well-being. The last three chapters of this text provide an in-depth look at these strategies. For now, we raise the awareness of the need to increase one's awareness of the nature of burnout, its contributing factors, and the real possibility that you may be currently in the grips of burnout.

Self-Assessment

The first step in addressing the potential for or existence of burnout is for counselors to engage in self-reflection and assessment.

The Maslach Burnout Inventory-Human Services Survey. One measure for the identification of the elements associated with burnout is the Maslach Burnout Inventory-Human Services Survey (Maslach & Jackson, 1981). This inventory has 22 items divided into three subscales specific to the elements of burnout: depersonalization, emotional exhaustion, and reduced personal accomplishment. The *depersonalization scale* consists of five items that measure the counselor's response toward clients that is unfeeling and impersonal. The *emotional exhaustion scale* consists of nine items that measure "feelings of being emotionally overextended and exhausted by one's work" (Maslach et al., 1996, p. 194). The *personal accomplishment scale* consists of eight items and measures self-efficacy and feelings of achievement.

Each of the items is scaled from 0 to 6, where respondents identify the frequency of specific feelings or attitudes. For example, one item on the instrument, "I don't really care what happens to [clients]," is scaled from 0 (never) to 6 (every day). The instrument is scored in such a way that higher scores on the emotional exhaustion and depersonalization scales indicate higher levels of burnout, while the opposite is true of the personal accomplishment scale.

The Counselor Burnout Scale. The Maslach Burnout Inventory-Human Services Survey (Maslach & Jackson, 1981) is useful in gaining some insight into the experience of burnout among counselors. However, the MBI does not explicitly assess burnout unique to those serving as professional counselors. As a result, the Counselor Burnout Inventory (CBI) was developed by Lee et al. (2007).

In addition to targeting burnout as specific to the professional experience of counselors, the CBI expands the theoretical framework, including organizational sources of burnout. The CBI (Lee et al., 2007) is a 20-item measure of burnout that has counselors rate items along five dimensions: (1) exhaustion, (2) negative work environment, (3) devaluing client, (4) incompetence, and (5) deterioration of personal life using a 1 (never true) to 5 (always true) Likert scale format.

The first dimension, "exhaustion," is assessed by four items that focus on both physical and emotional exhaustion that result from the counselor's job experience. One item, for example, states, "Due to my job as a counselor, I feel tired most of the time." The second dimension, labeled "negative work environment," employs four CBI items to tap the counselor's attitudes and feelings toward his work environment. For example, one item states, "I feel frustrated with the system in my workplace." The third dimension, labeled "devaluing client," employs four items to assess the counselor's attitude and perception of her relationship with the client. An example of the type of item presented in this cluster is "I have become callous toward clients." "Incompetence," the fourth dimension, targets the counselor's feelings of incompetence with four items, such as, "I am not confident in my counseling skills." The final dimension, labeled "deterioration of personal life," employed four items, focusing on the deterioration of the counselor's personal life with items such as, "I feel like I do not have enough time to engage in personal interests."

Informal self-monitoring. Either of the above assessment measures provides a valid, reliable assessment of a counselor's level of burnout. However, one need not turn to a formal assessment tool to monitor changes in behavior, energy levels, social engagement, and physical health, which may be indicative of burnout. Exercise 5.1 invites you to review a number of markers that may indicate the onset of burnout.

EXERCISE 5.1

Monitoring Early Indicators of Burnout

Directions: The following are a number of behaviors that could serve as early warning signs of the existence of burnout. It is suggested that you schedule regular self-assessments as a way of monitoring your own level of health and well-being.

Targets for Risk Assessment	Frequently	Occasionally	Rarely	Never
I find it difficult to find time to eat lunch.				
I find it challenging to find time to exercise.				
When I leave work, I feel physically exhausted.				
I don't want to go out and socialize after work.				
I do not have an interest in engaging in activities or hobbies I used to enjoy.				

Targets for Risk Assessment	Frequently	Occasionally	Rarely	Never
I do not read for enjoyment.				
I often dread going to work.				
I feel unappreciated/undervalued at work.				
I question the effectiveness of what I do at work.				
I find little professional satisfaction or fulfillment.				
I disengage from professional interactions.				
I rarely participate in causes I used to value.				
I often feel emotionally flat.				
I do not engage in activities that foster a more significant, "spiritual" connection.				
I find it difficult to take breaks (including eating lunch) at work.				
I have little to no interest in engaging work colleagues as support.				
I find that I am experiencing physical problems like stomachaches, headaches, lingering colds, and general aches and pains more than usual.				
I find myself annoyed and irritated at being asked to engage with regular assignments.				

Recognition of both the risk of burnout and the early indications that one is starting down that path is essential to ethical, effective practice. While recognition and awareness are necessary, they are not sufficient to ensure ethical practice. Counselors must engage in self-care to maintain their psychological wellness to support their ethical and effective practice. Chapters 8, 9, and 10 outline steps that can be taken to support a counselor's health and emotional well-being.

KEYSTONES

- The stress experienced as a counselor can affect not only the counselor's personal life but also interfere with the professional functioning of his or her clients (Skosnik et al., 2000).

- The need to monitor a counselor's emotional and physical health, as well as practice wellness, is clearly stated in our codes of ethics.

- Burnout is by nature an insidious experience, having no clear beginning or ending, but slowly increasing its damage over time. Burnout appears to be the cumulative effect of witnessing and engaging with humans who are suffering (O'Brien, 2011; Webb, 2011).

- Maslach (1982) identified three distinct elements of burnout: depersonalization, emotional exhaustion, and evaluating oneself negatively.

- There is no one single cause of burnout. However, some factors have been found to contribute to the occurrence of burnout. Factors such as long hours, heavy caseloads, and isolation within the work setting, along with unrealistic role expectations, have all been reported to contribute to the development of burnout (Evans & Villavisanis, 1997; Schaufeli, 2003).

- The work of counselors is genuinely emotionally draining, making them vulnerable to burnout (Bakker et al., 2006; Skovholt, 2001).

- The first step in addressing the potential for or existence of burnout is for counselors to engage in self-reflection and assessment.

ADDITIONAL RESOURCES

In Print

Center for Mental Health in Schools at UCLA. (2008). *Understanding and minimizing staff burnout.* Los Angeles, CA: Author.

DeAngelis, T. (2002, July/August). Normalizing practitioners' stress. *Monitor on Psychology, 33*(7), 62–64.

Kim, H., & Stoner, M. (2008). Burnout and turnover intention among social workers: Effect of role, stress, job autonomy, and social support. *Administration in Social Work, 32*(3), 5–25.

Leiter, M. P., Bakker, A. B., & Maslach, C. (Eds.). (2014). *Burnout at work: A psychological perspective.* New York, NY: Psychology Press.

Warnath, C. F., & Shelton, J. L. (1976). The ultimate disappointment: The burned-out counselor. *Personnel and Guidance Journal, 55,* 172–175.

Web Based

ACA's Taskforce on Counselor Wellness and Impairment. (n.d.). Retrieved from http://www.counseling.org/wellness_taskforce/index.htm

Breakthrough burnout: A self-reflection of one clinician's experience. (n.d.). Retrieved from http://www.blackgirlinom.com/publication-articles/2017/8/breaking-through-burnout-how-to-bring-your-wellness-to-work

A counselor's journey back from burnout. (n.d.). Retrieved from https://ct.counseling.org/2017/04/a-counselors-journey-back-from-burnout/

REFERENCES

American Counseling Association (ACA). (2014). *ACA Code of Ethics.* Retrieved from https://www.schoolcounselor.org/asca/media/asca/Ethics/EthicalStandards2016.pdf

American School Counseling Association (ASCA). (2016). *ASCA Ethical Standards for School Counselors.* Retrieved from https://www.schoolcounselor.org/asca/media/asca/Ethics/EthicalStandards2016.pdf

American Mental Health Counselors Association. (2015). AMHCA Code of Ethics. Retrieved from http://www.amhca.org/learn/ethics

Bakker, A. B., Van der Zee, K. I., Lewig, K. A., & Dollard, M. F. (2006). The relationship between the big five personality factors and burnout: A study among volunteer counselors. *The Journal of Social Psychology, 126,* 31–50.

Bardhoshi, G., Schweinle, A., & Duncan, K. (2014). Understanding the impact of school factors on school counselor burnout: A mixed-methods study. *The Professional Counselor, 4*(5), 426–443.

Deighton, R., Gurris, N., & Traue, H. (2007). Factors affecting burnout and compassion fatigue in psychotherapists treating torture survivors: Is the therapist's attitude to working through trauma relevant? *Journal of Traumatic Stress, 20*(1), 63–75.

Evans, T. D., & Villavisanis, R. (1997). Encouragement exchange: Avoiding therapist burnout. *The Family Journal: Counseling and Therapy for Couples and Families, 5,* 342–345.

Fothergill, A., Edwards, D., & Burnard. P. (2004). Stress, burnout, coping and stress management in psychiatrists: Findings from a systematic review. *International Journal of Social Psychiatry, 50,* 54–65.

Gladding, S. T. (2011). *The counseling dictionary: Concise definitions of frequently used terms.* Upper Saddle River, NJ: Pearson Education.

Hamann, D. L., & Gordon, D. G. (2000). Burnout: An occupational hazard. *Music Educators Journal, 87,* 34–39.

Kottler, J. A. (1989). *On Being a Therapist.* San Francisco, CA: Jossey-Bass Publisher.

Lambie, G. W. (2002). The contribution of ego development level to degree of burnout in school counselors. *Dissertation Abstracts International, 63,* 508.

Larson, D. G. (1993). *The helper's journey.* Champaign, IL: Research Press.

Lee, S. M., Cho, S. H., Kissinger, D., & Ogle, N. T. (2010). A typology of burnout in professional counselors. *Journal of Counseling & Development, 40,* 142–154.

Lee, S. M., Baker, C. R., Cho, S. H., Heckathorn, D. E., Holland, M.W., Newgent, R. A., ... Yu, K. (2007). Development and initial psychometrics of the counselor burnout inventory. *Measurement and Evaluation in Counseling and Development, 40*(3), 142–154.

Maslach, C. (1982). *Burnout: The cost of caring.* Englewood Cliffs, NJ: Prentice-Hall.

Maslach, C. & Jackson, S. E. (1986). *Maslach burnout inventory manual* (2nd ed.). Paolo Alto, CA: Consulting Psychologists Press.

Maslach, C., Jackson S., & Leiter, M. P. (1996). *Maslach burnout inventory* (3rd ed.). Palo Alto, CA: Consulting Psychologists Press.

Maslach Burnout Inventory. (1997). *MBI manual* (2nd ed.). Palo Alto, CA: Consulting Psychologists Press.

Maslach, C., Schaufeli, W. B., & Leiter, M. P. (2001). Job burnout. *Annual Review of Psychology, 52,* 397–422.

McCarthy, C., Van Horn Kerne, V., Calfa, N. A., Lambert, R. G., & Guzman, M. (2010). An exploration of school counselors' demands and resources: Relationship to stress, biographic, and caseload characteristics. *Professional School Counseling, 13*(3), 146–158.

McMullen, M. B., & Krantz, M. (1988). Burnout in daycare workers: The effects of learned helplessness and self-esteem. *Child and Youth Care Quarterly, 17,* 275–280.

Morse, G., Salyers, M., Rollins, A., Monroe-DeVita, M., & Pfahler, C. (2012). *Administrative Policy in Mental Health and Mental Health Services Research, 39*(5), 341–352.

O'Brien, J. M. (2011). Wounded healer: Psychotherapist's grief over a client's death. *Professional Psychology Research and Practice, 42,* 236–243.

Osborn, C. J. (2004). Seven salutary suggestions for counselor stamina. *Journal of Counseling & Development, 82*(3), 319–328.

Schaufeli, W. B. (2003). Past performance and future perspectives of burnout research. *South African Journal of Industrial Psychology, 29,* 1–15.

Skosnik, P. D.; Chatterton, R. T., Swisher, T., & Park, S. (2000). Modulation of attentional inhibition by norepinephrine and cortisol after psychological stress. *International Journal of Psychophysiology, 36*(1), 59–68.

Skovholt, T. M. (2001) *The resilient practitioner. Burnout prevention and self-care strategies for counselors, therapists, teachers, and health professionals.* Boston, MA: Allyn & Bacon.

Webb, K. M. (2011). Care of others and self: A suicidal patient's impact on the psychologist. *Professional Psychology: Research and Practice, 42,* 215.

Whealin, J. M., Batzer, W. B., Morgan, C. A., Detwiler, H. F., Schunurr, P. P., & Medman, M. J. (2007). Cohesion, burnout, and past trauma in tri-service medical and support personnel. *Military Medicine, 172,* 266–272.

6

Secondary (Vicarious) Traumatization

I would wake up in the middle night, totally drenched in sweat and shaking. I am overwhelmed by the sounds of children screaming.

—Dr. Alison N.

Secondary or vicarious traumatization is a process that can result in changes in a counselor's psychological, physical, and spiritual well-being. It would not be unexpected to find that counselors who work in the area of crisis and trauma counseling are vulnerable to the experience of secondary traumatization. The truth, however, is that all counselors will encounter clients who share their own stories of crisis and trauma, and it is unrealistic to assume that any counselor is insulated from the effects of listening to stories of such pain and trauma. Bride (2004), for example, found that between 82% and 94% of clients seeking treatment had experienced some form of trauma. As such, it is very likely that counselors will be exposed to the traumatic experiences of their clients, and as such, there is potential for counselors to be negatively impacted (Foreman, 2018). Dunkley and Whelan (2006) estimated the prevalence rate of vicarious traumatization to be 45.9% among counselors.

The current chapter describes the experience of secondary (vicarious) traumatization and its effect on one's personal and professional life. After reading this chapter, you should be able to complete the following:

a. Explain the characteristics associated with a counselor's experience of secondary (vicarious) traumatization.

b. Describe the various conditions or factors that increase one's risk of experiencing secondary (vicarious) traumatization.

c. Identify strategies for assessing the possibility of secondary (vicarious) traumatization.

d. Understand the concept of vicarious post-traumatic growth (PTG).

Embracing Client Trauma as Your Own

Research (e.g., Bride, 2004; Dunkley & Whelan, 2006) has been clear in noting that exposure to the explicit and often graphic accounts of traumatic experiences can result in a counselor's vicarious engagement with trauma. The term, vicarious traumatization, used to describe the consequences of a counselor's experience with client trauma, was coined by McCann and Pearlman (1990a). The ongoing engagement with clients who are struggling with their crises or who may have survived personal trauma can take a severe toll on the counselor. According to McCann and Pearlman (1990b), "Persons who work with victims may experience profound psychological effects, effects that can be disruptive and painful for the helper and can persist for months or years after work with traumatized persons" (p. 133).

Vicarious traumatization is the result of multiple contacts. It is cumulative and unfolds over time. While vicarious traumatization develops over time, the symptoms can appear quite suddenly (Sabin-Farrell & Turpin, 2003) and can extend well beyond the boundaries of counseling sessions, affecting the counselor's personal life (Moulden & Firestone, 2007). Vicarious traumatization results in dramatic changes in the way the therapist experiences him or herself, others, and the environment (McCann & Pearlman, 1990a).

While less intense, the symptoms of vicarious trauma are similar to experiences of primary trauma (Catanese, 2010). Counselors caught in the grips of secondary traumatization can experience intense images and other PTSD symptomology. Secondary or vicarious traumatization can result not only in feelings of sadness, grief, irritability, and mood swings (Catanese, 2010) but also in profound changes in the counselor's core sense of self (Pearlman & Saakvitne, 1995). Those experiencing secondary/vicarious traumatization note that their view of issues, such as safety, esteem, trust and dependency, control, and intimacy, has been altered (Pearlman & Saakvitne, 1995). Case Illustration 6.1 provides a very intimate look at the debilitating effect of secondary traumatization.

CASE ILLUSTRATION 6.1

Dr. Alison N.

I have been a school counselor for over 20 years. I have worked with students who have presented with issues ranging from the normative challenges of friendship conflicts, through to those exhibiting debilitating anxiety and even depression. But the events of these past few months have been something that I never expected.

It was October, and the fifth-grade students were scheduled to take a field trip. The details of what happened are still sketchy, but the bottom line was that the bus carrying the students had a blowout and as a result careened off the highway, turning over on the side of the highway and bursting into flames. My God, just talking about this is making me want to cry. Somehow, miraculously, no one was seriously injured. I saw pictures of the bus, and it is beyond me how anyone escaped without significant injury or even death.

It is now two months since the accident, but the children are still coming to my office to talk about the crash. They seem just to want to talk about it, over and over.

The stories are very similar. They describe, in detail, the sound of the blowout, the smell, the sound of the brake locking and squealing, and the feeling of being thrown about inside the bus. Many will describe seeing blood on other students or themselves. A number of the students hit their mouths on the back of seats and split a lip or lost a tooth. Two students cut their foreheads, requiring stitches, and they had blood all over their faces.

But the thing that makes me want to cry is when they describe the sounds of the accident. Each one of the students I have seen talks about the squeal of the tires, the horrible crunching sound of the bus rolling into the ditch but most graphically... the screaming.

I can't get the image and the sound out of my mind. As I am talking with my students, I can see their little faces and sense the horror they feel even as they share their stories. I have a difficult time not losing it in front of them. I can "hear" the chaos and the screaming. I can't shake it. It is as if I was on that bus.

I can't eat. I am afraid of going to sleep. I just know I'll have nightmares. I dread seeing the students coming into my office, knowing that it is going to start all over. I am a mess; I just don't feel safe. I know it's crazy, but I can't get over it.

Conditions of Vulnerability

Developing an awareness of those factors or conditions that increase a counselor's vulnerability to experiencing secondary (vicarious) trauma can serve as the first step to prevention and protection. Secondary trauma arises out of empathetic engagement with distressed clients (Figley, 1995; Trippany, Kress, & Wilcoxon, 2004).

It is expected that the nature of the work a counselor does, and the degree in which he is engaged with clients experiencing trauma, will increase the risk of that counselor experiencing secondary trauma. In addition to the nature of the work performed, the population served, and the context within which services are provided, personal characteristics of the counselor can contribute to the risk level experienced (Pearlman & Saakvitne, 1995). Vicarious traumatization has been found to be connected to personality variables, such as personal identity, individual worldview, and emotional style (Pearlman & Saakvitne, 1995), and previous personal trauma history (Resick, 2000; Rosenthal, 2000).

Pearlman and McKay (n.d.) suggest that each of the following personal factors can contribute to a counselor's elevated level of risk for experiencing secondary (vicarious) traumatization.

Personal stress management style. According to Pearlman and McKay (n.d), those who tend to employ avoidance strategies to manage their stress experience may be more susceptible to vicarious traumatization. This is contrasted with those who tend to seek support and who actively try to solve their problems.

Personal history. Personal experience with trauma does not automatically make one more vulnerable to the experience of secondary (vicarious) trauma. However, it seems that those whose histories facilitate their identification and deep empathy with clients who share their trauma have a heightened risk for secondary (vicarious) trauma.

Personal stress. As might be expected, counselors who are already coping with a great deal of personal stress place themselves at higher risk for secondary (vicarious) trauma.

Work style. Counselors who tend to take their work home and hold unrealistic expectations and a sense of responsibility may be more vulnerable to the experience of vicarious (secondary) traumatization. Similarly, those who tend to blur the boundaries of the "I-thou" counseling relationship, failing to keep appropriate professional objectivity, are also at higher risk. Case Illustration 6.2 provides an example of how some personal factors may affect the counseling relationship.

CASE ILLUSTRATION 6.2

I Can Handle This. Can't I?

I have been working in the counseling field for over 5 years now and have always prided myself on being able to leave my work and my client's issues in the office. I don't want to burden my partner with my feelings, and I lost touch with my colleagues in my old supervision group, so I don't discuss anything with anyone. But up until now, things seemed to be going well. However, lately, I feel edgy and out-of-sorts during some of my counseling sessions, especially the sessions dealing with emotional abuse.

This is ridiculous. I can handle this! I've helped my partner numerous times when she needed to work through her history of emotional abuse. I know what I'm doing, and I shouldn't need help, or do I? I'm sure I'm fine. I just got married, and this should be one of the best times of my life. I wonder why those sessions are bothering me.

Additional factors that can place a counselor at risk for secondary (vicarious) traumatization are found in the following exercise (Exercise 6.1). While the items listed in Exercise 6.1 were initially presented as factors that promote wellness (see Saakvitne, Pearlman, L.A., & the Staff of the Traumatic Stress Institute, 1996), it is suggested that their absence may signify increased vulnerability.

EXERCISE 6.1

Assessing Vulnerability

Directions: The following items have been adapted from the self-care assessment worksheet developed by Saakvitne, K. W., Pearlman, L. A., & the Staff of the Traumatic Stress Institute (1996). It is suggested that you review the items listed as a method for assessing the degree to which you engage in these self-care activities.

5 = Frequently
4 = Occasionally
3 = Rarely
2 = Never
1 = It never occurred to me

Physical Self-Care
____ How often do you eat regular meals (e.g., breakfast, lunch, and dinner)?
____ The degree to which you eat "healthy" food.
____ How often do you exercise?
____ Get regular medical care for prevention
____ Engage in physical activities (e.g., dance or play sports) that are fun
____ Sleep at least 8 hours
____ Take vacations, even mini-day trips

Psychological Self-Care
____ Make time for self-reflection
____ Meditate
____ Read literature that is unrelated to work
____ Experience new things that challenge your intelligence
____ Say "no" when extra demands are requested

Emotional Self-Care
____ Spend time with others whose company you enjoy
____ Give yourself pats on the back for a job well done
____ Express your emotions
____ Laugh
____ Love and be loved

Spiritual Self-Care
____ Connect with a spiritual community
____ Find and be open to sources of inspiration
____ Appreciate nature
____ Meditate
____ Pray
____ Engage with meaningful "causes"

Workplace or Professional Self-Care
___ Take a break during the workday (e.g., lunch)
___ Take time to chat with coworkers
___ Set limits with your clients and colleagues
___ Balance your caseload so that no one day or part of a day is "too much"
___ Arrange your work space so that it is comfortable and comforting
___ Negotiate for your needs (benefits, pay raise)

Balance
___ Strive for balance within your work life and workday
___ Strive for balance among work, family, relationships, play, and rest
___ Strive for balance in physical, psychological, social-emotional, and spiritual dimensions of your life

Source: Adapted from Saakvitne, K. W., Pearlman, L. A., & the Staff of the Traumatic Stress Institute (1996). Transforming the pain: A workbook on vicarious traumatization. New York, NY: W.W. Norton.

Recognition: Essential for Intervention and Prevention

Strategies to employ to reduce the risk and potential of experiencing secondary (vicarious) trauma, as well as strategies to engage as interventions when in the state of secondary trauma, are presented in the last three chapters of this book. However, before the engagement of any prevention or intervention strategies, counselors must increase their awareness of the possible threats and indications of secondary (vicarious) trauma. Monitoring one's state of physical and emotional well-being is both an ethical mandate (e.g., ACA, 2014, C.2.g; ASCA, 2016, B.3.f) and a practical step to addressing the risk of secondary traumatization. Table 6.1 provides a list of some of the common signs or symptoms associated with vicarious trauma. The list has been adapted from the ACA's Vicarious Trauma—Fact Sheet #9 (ACA, n.d.).

In addition to such an "informal" checklist, counselors are encouraged to employ standardized instruments explicitly developed for the assessment of secondary trauma. A commonly used method of measurement for vicarious trauma is the Traumatic Stress Institute Belief Scale—Revision L (TSI-BSL). The TSI-BLS consists of an 80-item questionnaire measuring levels of disruption among five separate domains of safety, trust, control, esteem, and intimacy (Jenkins & Baird, 2002). The Traumatic Stress Institute Life Events Checklist (TSI-LEC) is another instrument used for measuring vicarious trauma. The TSI-LEC attempts to identify the added vulnerability that an individual professional might have to the onset of vicarious trauma because of the personal trauma that may have occurred over the course of their own lives (Bride, Radey, & Figley, 2007). One final instrument widely used in the field is the Secondary Traumatic Stress Scale (STSS). The 17-item STSS was developed specifically for those within the helping professions. It contains three subscales (intrusion, avoidance, arousal) and assesses the frequency of STS symptoms experienced by clinicians in the past 7 days using a 5-point, Likert-type response format (Bride, Robinson, Yegidis, & Figley, 2004).

TABLE 6.1 Signs of Secondary Traumatization

Physical	• Physical ailments—such as headaches or migraines, dizziness, fatigue, chest pain, breathing difficulties, and stomach and digestive issues • Difficulty sleeping
Cognitive/Behavioral	• Hyperarousal • Intolerance • Disengagement from previously enjoyed activities • Impulsivity • Nightmares/reexperiencing • Avoidance of situations/cues connected to the trauma
Interpersonal	• Social withdrawal • Irritation in relationships • Interpersonal conflicts • Interpersonally disconnected • Withdrawal and isolation from colleagues • Difficulty having rewarding relationships
Mood	• Anxiety • Depression • Dread • Despair
Beliefs and Values	• Questioning of the meaning of life and value of the profession • Reduction in trust • Increased sense of vulnerability • Loss of idealism • Questioning frame of reference, identity, worldview, and spirituality • Disruption in self-capacity (ability to maintain a positive sense of self, ability to modulate strong affect, and ability to maintain an inner sense of connection) • Disruption in needs, beliefs, and relationships (safety, trust, esteem, control, and intimacy)

Adapted from the American Counseling Association's Vicarious Trauma—Fact Sheet #9 (ACA, n.d.).

The Upside (?) to Trauma Exposure

The literature is clear. Exposure to client trauma can threaten a counselor's professional functioning and personal well-being. To suggest that there may be some upside for a counselor engaged with client trauma may seem counterintuitive. Attempts have been made to understand the positive change individuals and therapists experience as a result of their struggles in processing trauma work (Manning-Jones, de Terte, & Stephens, 2015).

Those engaged in researching PTG (e.g., Bartoskova, 2017; Morris, Shakespeare-Finch, Rieck, & Newberry, 2005; Tedeschi & Calhoun, 2004) note that counselors can experience positive change as a result of struggling with the challenges of trauma. The position is that a traumatic experience can cause a positive reevaluation of that worldview (Arnold, Calhoun, Tedeschi, & Cann, 2005; Tedeschi & Calhous, 2004). Case Illustration 6.3 provides an example of how a counselor can experience positive growth after exposure to trauma.

CASE ILLUSTRATION 6.3

What Is Life's Purpose?

Vida is a college counselor at a Christian private college. She entered into a therapeutic relationship with Brittany, a sophomore who was a resident hall assistant. Brittany was the first witness to a student (and a friend) who completed suicide in one of the rooms in the hall. This tragic event had a significant effect on the residents and the college community but most severely on Brittany. Brittany reported struggling with severe emotional distress, flashbacks, and a sense of hopelessness for the future. Brittany struggled with understanding why we exist in life as humans and why bad things happen to good people. She asked, "Why do humans suffer, and what role does God play in all of that?"

The questions raised by her client, along with the reflections shared in session, affected Vida. While engaging with her supervisor, Vida became aware of the effect her work with Brittany was having on her world view. The existential perspective that she brought to her work with Brittany provided a lens for her own reflection on the meaning of life, of her existence. Vida elected to reflect many of the same therapeutic questions that she posed to Brittany. Her reflections helped her increase awareness and appreciation of life, establish and maintain meaningful relationships, build a strong spiritual connection by studying the Bible with other believers, and live each day as though it was the last one!

According to Tedeschi, Calhoun, and Groleau (2015), PTG is reflective of greater psychological and cognitive development, emotional adjustment, and life awareness. It is posited that PTG can result in three types of changes: (1) changes in self-perception, (2) changes in interpersonal relationships, and (3) changes in life philosophy (Tedeschi & Calhoun, 1996). While research (e.g., Bartoskova, 2017) supports the notion that counselors experiencing client trauma may experience PTG, more research, especially about the process underlying such growth, is needed (see the literature review by Bartoskova, 2015).

KEYSTONES

- Bride (2004), for example, found that between 82% and 94% of clients seeking treatment had experienced some form of trauma.

- It is very likely that counselors will be exposed to the traumatic experiences of their clients, and as such, there is potential for counselors to be negatively affected (Foreman, 2018).

- McCann and Pearlman (1990b) noted that "persons who work with victims may experience profound psychological effects, effects that can be disruptive and painful for the helper and can persist for months or years after work with traumatized persons."

- Vicarious traumatization develops over time; the symptoms can appear quite suddenly (Sabin-Farrell & Turpin, 2003) and can extend well beyond the boundaries of counseling sessions, affecting the counselor's personal life.

- Counselors caught in the grips of secondary traumatization can experience intense images and other PTSD symptomology. Secondary or vicarious traumatization can result not only in feelings of sadness, grief, irritability, and mood swings (Catanese, 2010) but also in profound changes in the counselor's core sense of self (Pearlman & Saakvitne, 1995).

- Vicarious traumatization has been found to be connected to personality variables, such as personal identity, worldview, and emotional style (Pearlman & Saakvitne, 1995), and previous personal trauma history (Resick, 2000; Rosenthal, 2000).

- Counselors are encouraged to employ standardized instruments explicitly developed for the assessment of secondary trauma, such as (a) TSI-BSL, (b) TSI-LEC, and (c) STSS.

- Those engaged in researching PTG (e.g., Bartoskova, 2017; Tedeschi & Calhoun, 2004) note that counselors can experience positive change as a result of struggling with the challenges of trauma.

- While research (e.g., Bartoskova, 2017) supports the notion that counselors experiencing client trauma may experience PTG, more research, especially about the process underlying such growth, is needed.

ADDITIONAL RESOURCES

In Print

Hernandez, P., Gangsei, D., & Engstrom, D. (2007). Vicarious resilience: A new concept in work with those who survive. *Family Process, 46*(2), 229–241.

Pearlman, L. A., & Caringi, J. (2009). Living and working self-reflectively to address vicarious trauma. In C. A. Courtois & J. D. Ford (Eds.), *Treating complex traumatic stress disorders: An evidence-based guide* (pp. 202–224). New York, NY: Guilford Press.

Saakvitne, K. W., Gamble, S. G., Pearlman, L. A., & Lev, B. T. (2000). *Risking connection: A training curriculum for working with survivors of childhood abuse.* Lutherville, MD: Sidran Foundation and Press.

Saakvitne, K. W., Pearlman, L. A., & the Staff of the Traumatic Stress Institute (1996). *Transforming the pain: A workbook on vicarious traumatization.* New York, NY: W.W. Norton.

Web Based

Figley Institute: Figley Institute offers cutting-edge training and continuing education programs to those who provide relief to emotionally traumatized individuals, families, businesses, and communities: http://www.figleyinstitute.com/indexMain.html

Pearlman, L. A., & McKay, L. (n.d.). Understanding and addressing vicarious trauma. Online training module four. Retrieved from https://headington-institute.org/files/vtmoduletemplate2_ready_v2_85791.pdf

The Trauma Research, Education, and Training Institute, Inc. (TREATI): Provides information and training to increase the abilities of mental health and social service workers to provide effective, ethical treatment for survivors of traumatic life experiences: http://ww3.treati.org/

REFERENCES

American Counseling Association. (2014). ACA Code of ethics. Retrieved from https://www.counseling.org/knowledge-center/ethics

American Counseling Association. (n.d.). *Vicarious trauma—Fact sheet #9.* Retrieved from https://www.counseling.org/docs/trauma-disaster/fact-sheet-9--vicarious-trauma.pdf

American School Counselor Association. (2016). ASCA ethical standards for school counselors. https://www.schoolcounselor.org/asca/media/asca/Ethics/EthicalStandards2016.pdf.

Arnold, D., Calhoun, L. G., Tedeschi, R., & Cann, A. (2005). Vicarious posttraumatic growth in psychotherapy. *Journal of Humanistic Psychology, 45,* 239–263.

Bartoskova, L. (2015). Research into post-traumatic growth in therapists: A critical literature review. *Counselling Psychology Review, 30*(3), 57–68.

Bartoskova, L. (2017). How do trauma therapists experience the effects of their trauma work, and are there common factors leading to post-traumatic growth? *Counselling Psychology Review, 32*(2), 30–45.

Bride, B. (2004). The impact of providing psychosocial services to traumatized populations. *Stress, Trauma, and Crisis, 7,* 29–64.

Bride, B. E., Radey, M., & Figley, C. R. (2007). Measuring compassion fatigue. *Clinical Social Work Journal, 35*(3), 155–163.

Bride, B. E., Robinson, M. M., Yegidis, B., & Figley, C. R. (2004). Development and validation of the secondary traumatic stress scale. *Research on Social Work Practice*, *14*, 27–35.

Catanese, S. A. (2010). *Traumatized by association: The risk of working sex crimes.* Retrieved from https://heinonline.org/HOL/LandingPage?handle=hein.journals/fedpro74&div=24&id=&page=

Dunkley, J., & Whelan, T. A. (2006). Vicarious traumatization: Current status and future directions. *British Journal of Guidance and Counselling*, *34*, 107–116.

Figley, C. R. (1995). Compassion fatigue as secondary traumatic stress disorder: An overview. In C. R. Figley (Ed.), *Compassion fatigue: Coping with secondary traumatic stress disorder in those who treat the traumatized* (pp. 1–20). Bristol, PA: Brunner/Mazel.

Foreman, T. (2018). Wellness, exposure to trauma, and vicarious traumatization: A pilot study. *Journal of Mental Health Counseling*, *40*(2), 142–155.

Jenkins, S. R., & Baird, S. (2002). Secondary traumatic stress and vicarious trauma: A validation study. *Journal of Traumatic Stress*, *15*(5), 423–432.

Manning-Jones, S., de Terte, I., & Stephens, C. (2015). Vicarious posttraumatic growth: A systematic literature review. *International Journal of Wellbeing*, *5*(2), 125–139.

McCann, I. L., & Pearlman, L. A. (1990a). *Psychological trauma and the adult survivor: Theory, therapy, and transformation.* New York, NY: Brunner/Mazel.

McCann, I. L., & Pearlman, L. A. (1990b). Vicarious traumatization: A framework for understanding the psychological effects of working with victims. *Journal of Traumatic Stress*, *3*(1), 131–149.

Moulden, H. M., & Firestone, P. (2007). Vicarious traumatization: The impact on therapists who work with sexual offenders. *Trauma Violence Abuse*, *8*(1), 67–83.

Morris, B. A., Shakespeare-Finch, J., Rieck, M., & Newbery, J. (2005). Multidimensional nature of posttraumatic growth in an Australian population. *Journal of Traumatic Stress*, *18*, 575–585.

Pearlman, L. A., & McKay, L. (n.d.). *Understanding and addressing vicarious trauma.* Retrieved from https://headington-institute.org/files/vtmoduletemplate2_ready_v2_85791.pdf

Pearlman, L. A., & Saakvitne, K. W. (1995). *Trauma and the therapist.* New York, NY: W.W. Norton.

Resick, P. (2000). *Stress and trauma.* Hove, UK: Psychology Press.

Rosenthal, B. S. (2000). Exposure to community violence in adolescence: Trauma symptoms. *Adolescence*, *35*, 271–284.

Saakvitne, Pearlman, & Staff of TSI/CAAP. (1996). *Transforming the pain: A workbook on vicarious traumatization.* New York: W. W. Norton.

Sabin-Farrell, R., & Turpin, G. (2003). Vicarious traumatization: Implications for the mental health of health workers? *Clinical Psychology Review*, *23*, 449–480.

Tedeschi, R. G., & Calhoun, L. G. (1996). The posttraumatic growth inventory: Measuring the positive legacy of trauma. *Journal of Traumatic Stress, 9*, 455–471.

Tedeschi, R. G., & Calhoun, L. G. (2004). Post-traumatic growth: Conceptual foundations and empirical evidence. *Psychological Inquiry, 15*, 1–18.

Tedeschi, R. G., Calhoun, L. G., & Groleau, J. M. (2015). Clinical applications of post-traumatic growth. In S. Joseph, Ed. *Positive psychology in practice: Promoting human flourishing in work, health, education, and everyday life* (2nd ed., pp. 503–518). Hoboken, NJ: John Wiley & Sons, Inc.

Trippany, R. L., Kress, V. E., & Wilcoxon, S. A. (2004). Preventing vicarious trauma: What counselors should know when working with trauma survivors. *Journal of Counseling and Development, 82*, 31–37.

Beyond Practical ... Ethical

I take care of everyone else; it's my job! I know that care is important, including self-care, and I emphasize that to my clients and the students I teach. I get it, I understand—so I'm not sure if there is anything more, or anything specifically, that I need to do for myself, right?

—Mikel, Second-Year Clinical Mental Health Counselor

You may be thinking that, of course, counselors understand that it is crucial for clients to work toward wellness and practice self-care. But how about counselors themselves? Is self-care more than just a good idea for counselors? Should it be a priority? The answer, one which is highlighted across our codes of ethics, is emphatically *yes*! Wellness and self-care are such a vital part of being a counselor that they are identified as part of the code of ethics for the ACA (2014, C. Introduction), the ASCA (2016, B.3.f.), the AMHCA (2015, Ch.), and the NASW (2017, 4.05.a.).

The current chapter discusses not only the practical importance of maintaining wellness as a practitioner but also the ethical responsibility and mandate directing us to such a wellness orientation. After reading this chapter, you should be able to complete the following:

a. Understand the importance of being aware of your well-being and how it can affect your effectiveness as an ethical counselor.

b. Describe the characteristics of an ethical counselor who is practicing wellness.

c. Identify the ethical standards expected of a professional counselor in terms of wellness.

Practical: Oxygen Mask on You and Then on Your Client

Counselors spend their work time listening to and supporting clients and students in their times of need. Sometimes the need is great, and the challenges are many, such as in the case of traumatized clients, while other times the issue and the need may be less taxing on the client and counselor alike. Regardless of the intensity of the issue and dynamic experienced, attending to our clients, listening for understanding, and experiencing the depth of empathy in the process of helping others through their journey will take a toll.

As described in the beginning chapters of this book, the role of a counselor is one that provides both the rewards *and* costs of walking with people during times when they are struggling. As noted in the previous chapters, mental health professionals and educators are among the highest of identified professionals to experience burnout, compassion fatigue, and secondary trauma. Factors such as high rates of stress, large caseloads, demands of the job, and ethical burdens can and do take their toll on a counselor's well-being (Morse, Salyers, Rollins, Monroe-DeVita, & Pfahler, 2012; Sang Min, Seong, Kissinger, & Ogle, 2010; Sowa & May, 1994).

Given these realities, it becomes clear that understanding the nature of burnout, compassion fatigue, and secondary trauma, as well as understanding the steps to be taken to reduce the probability of experiencing these threats is a given, a practical reality, for all who enter this profession. But it is more than just a practical concern; it is an ethical concern. Imagine going to a counselor who doesn't keep appointments, stares off in the distance as you are talking, or says, "Hey, do what you think is best—I'm not sure what to tell you." Chances are you would think that this person cannot possibly be helpful to you. You may even believe that this counselor needs to see her own counselor. And chances are you would be correct. Even in situations where a client is unaware of this level of counselor disengagement, the counselor must be self-aware and aware that under these conditions she will not only be less than effective but may violate a primary mandate of the Hippocratic Oath to "do no harm." Case Illustration 7.1 highlights the costs of counselor failure to attend to self-care.

CASE ILLUSTRATION 7.1

Maybe It Doesn't Matter

Kevin was running late, again. He hadn't been able to sleep well since the baby was born, and he had slept through his alarm. He would make his first appointment but not have time to prepare at all. As a professional counselor for 10 years, Kevin was confident with his knowledge and skill but lately was finding it harder to focus during sessions. He had been seeing his first client, Benny, for almost a year, and he felt he was making progress toward the goal they had established.

Through the session, Kevin fought off his sleepiness and felt his mind wandering and picturing his newborn. He knew he appeared to be engaged because Benny kept talking. He had mastered the head nod and "um-hmms" to show interest and maintain the flow of conversation. He thought the session went well, although he did feel relieved when Benny left at the end of the scheduled 45 minutes. He could catch a quick nap before his next client.

As Kevin closed the door following Benny's exit, Benny quietly mumbled to himself, "I don't understand why Kevin seemed so disinterested in what happened to me this week. I thought it was pretty important to the goal, but maybe I was wrong. He kept changing the topic and trying to hide his yawns. I guess what happened doesn't matter … maybe I don't matter."

As illustrated in the case, counselors may believe they present as engaged, interested, and helpful when, in fact, that may not be what the client perceives. Even more concerning is when counselors are either not aware of or do not acknowledge that they are not working effectively and can cause harm. Helping professionals need to recognize that their work includes the types of stress and pressure that can lead to burnout and ineffective treatment and aim to maintain personal mental health to provide the highest level of professional service and support (Everall & Paulson, 2004).

It may be easy for some to dismiss this concern, seeing it as a "luxury" to care for oneself. It is not a "luxury"; it is an ethical mandate. The ethical codes are clear in expecting professional counselors to monitor their own "emotional and physical health and practice wellness" to maintain professional effectiveness that is optimal (ASCA, 2016, B.3.f.). In addition, counselors are to "refrain from offering or providing professional services when impaired" (ACA, 2014, C.2.g.). Counselors may rationalize that their struggles are not that serious or that they are not negatively affecting their practice, and besides, they have so many clients, so many responsibilities … and … so many bills that there is no time for self-care.

Let's step back and consider that which we have most likely heard numerous times while traveling via airlines. The preflight instructions typically include a description of the oxygen mask that would drop from the overhead compartment given a loss of cabin pressure. Along with that description comes the following message, *put on your oxygen mask before helping others*—a simple, straightforward, and practical directive. You need to be able to breathe, have sufficient oxygen, to be able to assist another person. This same advice—that is, to take care of yourself—applies to the task of helping others within the counseling relationship. If you are not healthy and not fully operating to the best of your ability, how can you expect to help others to the extent that they need? Consider the factors in Exercise 7.1 that may affect your effectiveness in a counseling relationship.

What Makes an Impact?

Directions: Consider the following factors that may impact you and the helping relationship when you are not **maintaining** your physical or mental health. It may be helpful to discuss these issues with a colleague or supervisor. A few examples have been provided.

Factor	Impact on You	Impact on the Helping Relationship
Not enough sleep	Fatigue, lack of focus	Inadequate or inaccurate listening and comprehension of the client's needs
Extended worry about family issues	Stomach and digestive issues	Inability to keep appointments
Overextension of work tasks		
Lack of leisure or social time		
Not asking for, or accepting, supervision		
Other		
Other		

Hopefully, by completing Exercise 7.1, your awareness has increased for how important it is to maintain wellness as a professional counselor. Our ethical codes not only direct us to keep wellness in our focus but also give us guidance for what to do when we are not working to our optimal level of care.

Ethical: Standards, Codes, and Beyond

The prime directive for those serving as professional counselors is "to respect the dignity and promote the welfare of clients" (ACA, 2014, A.1.a). Factors ranging from fatigue to significant psychological distress not only challenge the professional's ability to perform competently but also give form to this prime directive. Not all incidents of counselor stress and distress pose a risk to their adherence to this prime directive or to their ability to perform competently. As noted by the ACA Task Force on Counselor Wellness and Impairment (ACA, 2002), "Therapeutic impairment occurs when there is a significant negative impact on a counselor's professional functioning, which compromises client care or poses the potential for harm to the client." Consider Case Illustration 7.2, a case of one school counselor who was positioned to harm or at least neglect her student and, indeed, harm herself.

CASE ILLUSTRATION 7.2

"Help!"

Kourtney loved being a school counselor! She was busy all day, and she made sure she saw all the students either individually, in groups, or in the cafeteria. She rarely had time to eat lunch, but she didn't even notice as she moved from meetings to classroom lessons to her more direct interactions with the students. As the only counselor in the building, she was in charge of the school-wide behavior programs, and she felt like it was her responsibility to make them run well.

Kourtney arrived at school by 7:00 a.m. and rarely got home before 6:00 p.m. She frequently had to do her paperwork and record keeping before and after school because she was nonstop during the day. She considered herself fortunate to have a spouse who was able to pick up her two young children from their after-school child-care program so she could stay a bit later before going home to cook dinner. She didn't realize she had been missing out on some of her children's activities until recently when her daughter asked her if she could finally come to one of the chorus concerts because she hadn't made the last three performances.

Kourtney started having difficulty sleeping because of thinking of all her responsibilities and not knowing how she was going to manage them all to the degree she felt necessary. After all, "they need me!" Between her total engagement with her work, her post-work "worry" about the children, and her pursuit of graduate work in hopes of becoming a licensed professional counselor, there was no time for self nor family.

As a result of not sleeping, not eating, and feeling torn about neglecting her family, Kourtney ran out of physical and psychic energy. She contracted a bad respiratory infection and had no choice but to stay home and go to the doctor. When she returned to work the next day, several teachers came by to ask what was wrong, telling Kourtney that they noticed that she wasn't her usual cheery self and was forgetting about meetings and student appointments; they asked if she was all right. Kourtney would typically have responded with something like "I'm fine"; however, she paused and then quietly sagged into a chair and said, "Help!"

When we take a look at the counselor in Case Illustration 7.2, it becomes clear that her belief that she had to do it all, that the children needed her 24-7 attention, resulted in her neglect of her family and her physical, mental, and spiritual well-being. It is easy to see how she could have reached the depleted state she did when she got sick and essentially waved the "white flag." These practices, and the absence of alternative self-care practice, not only threaten one's well-being but can also interfere with the ability to provide ethical, effective service. The import of this reality has led the American Psychological Association (APA) to direct its members to "refrain from initiating an activity when they know or should know that there is a substantial likelihood that their personal problems will prevent them from performing their work-related activities in a competent manner" (APA, 2017, Principle 2.06).

We are ethically bound to monitor our behavior and recognize when we need to obtain professional consultation or assistance, or limit, suspend, or terminate our work-related duties. This is made clear in the ASCA's Code of Ethics with it is directive for members to "seek physical or mental health support when needed to ensure professional competence" (ASCA, 2016, B.3.f, B.3.g). The steps that may be required include limiting, suspending, or terminating professional responsibilities (ACA, 2014, C.2.g.) until one is fully functioning.

While it is apparent that one should suspend practice if impaired, our ethics require that we take steps to reduce the likelihood of such action becoming the case. The ACA's ethical code guides counselors to "engage in self-care activities to maintain and promote their own emotional, physical, mental, and spiritual well-being" (ACA, 2014, C, Introduction). Without taking time for wellness and attempting to meet a high level of demands, physical, emotional, and even spiritual depletion are not far behind and with their appearance a failure to perform competently.

Beyond engaging in self-care, there are professional activities that provide the support necessary to reduce the chances of becoming impaired. Although we may feel alone and isolated, consultation, and supervision within the realms of confidentiality are viable strategies for maintaining personal and professional wellness and effectiveness. Consultation and ongoing supervision are not only "good ideas" but are also found within our ethical codes as directives and highlighted as essential for ethical practice (ACA, 2014, c.2.d.; ASCA, 2016, B.3.h; NASW, 2008, 4.05.b.).

Before leaving the discussion of supervision and consultation, it is important to note that as counselors, we are not only charged to monitor ourselves for well-being but also to monitor our colleagues for signs of impairment. Just as we are responsible for ensuring that we are not harming ourselves or our clients through neglect or ineffective actions, we are to make sure that our colleagues are aware of their own potentially harmful behavior. Calling our colleagues to practice self-care and confronting their neglect of that self-care when such neglect affects the performance of their professional duties is also our ethical mandate (ACA, 2014, C.2.g.).

From Knowing to Doing

Understanding the need, as a professional counselor, to engage in self-care is undoubtedly an essential first step to maintaining well-being and ethical practice. Owning the practical and ethical implications of failure to engage in self-care is necessary but not sufficient for all counselors. Counselors must give form to that understanding and that ownership by developing and engaging a plan of self-care. If we return to our case of the school counselor, Kourtney, who needs help, we see how strategies of self-care and professional support can result in increased personal well-being and professional competence (see Case Illustration 7.3).

I'm OK. You're OK

Kourtney was doing all she thought she needed to do by herself and in the process not paying any attention to her well-being. She hit a wall, both personally and profession-ally, by getting sick and feeling she had failed her school community and her family. Kourtney's principal knew she was a dedicated and hardworking school counselor and recognized that she was not practicing self-care and was headed toward burnout. He requested a meeting with her to set realistic goals for the rest of the school year and suggested that Kourtney meet with the counselors in the other schools in the district for peer supervision.

Kourtney gratefully followed through and met with the other counselors, who, not surprisingly, were experiencing many of the same thoughts and feelings that Kourtney had. Together, they created a counselor job description and an annual calendar of tasks to address many of the organizational issues that were high demand and caus-ing great stress. In addition, they brainstormed ways that they could help each other to decrease their stress and increase self-care.

The district counselors requested that the administration support their plan to meet biweekly for peer supervision during the last hour of the school day. In addi-tion, the counselors planned on doing a fun activity together after the last meeting of the month. And, finally, they realized that the entire school community would benefit from self-care and set about to develop a school-wide unit on mindfulness. Kourtney added a meditation group time at her school on three mornings a week before the students arrived. She also set her schedule to arrive an hour later in the morning and leave at least an hour earlier at the end of the day so that she saw her family and was included in their lives to a greater degree. Within a week, Kourtney was smiling more and feeling like she had support and that she was doing an optimal job in every as-pect of her life. Her next goal is to get a break and lunch every day!

Now that you have an idea of the importance of self-care as a cornerstone for your well-being and your professional efficacy as an ethical counselor, you are invited to reflect on how you might use the ethical directives of supervision and consultation in Exercise 7.2.

Using Supervision and Consultation

Directions: Consider the ethical responsibilities of using supervision and consulta-tion. Reflect on how you might use these ethical directives for your well-being and the well-being of fellow counselors. Examples are provided.

Ethical Responsibility	How to Implement?
Supervision for self and fellow counselors	Connect with other counselors in the work setting or different local settings.
Consultation for self and fellow counselors	Ask for feedback and input from professional colleagues.

KEYSTONES

- Self-care and a focus on wellness is an ethical expectation for the professional counselor.

- Lack of physical, mental, or spiritual well-being can affect a counselor's personal and professional life.

- Counselors who are not functioning well or who are impaired have an ethical duty to limit or stop professional services and seek help.

- Consultation and supervision are expected and help maintain professional efficacy.

- Counselors are ethically charged to monitor their well-being and to pursue self-care.

ADDITIONAL RESOURCES

In Print

Carroll, L., Gilroy, P. J., & Murra, J. (1999). The moral imperative: Self-care for women psychotherapists. *Women & Therapy, 22,* 133–143.

Norcross, J. C., (2000). Psychotherapist self-care: Practitioner-tested, research-informed strategies. *Professional Psychology Research and Practice, 31*(6), 710–713.

Wise, E. H., & Barnett, J. E. (2016). Self-care for psychologists. In J. C. Norcross, G. R. VandenBos, D. K. Freedheim, & L. F. Campbell (Eds.), *APA handbooks in psychology. APA handbook of clinical psychology: Education and profession* (pp. 209–222). Washington, DC: American Psychological Association.

Stone, C. (2017). *School counseling principles: Ethics and law* (4th ed.)

Web Based

ACA https://www.counseling.org/

ASCA https://www.schoolcounselor.org/

AMHCA https://www.amhca.org/

APA https://www/apa.org

NASW https://www/socialworkers.org/

REFERENCES

American Counseling Association (ACA). (2002). *Taskforce on counselor wellness and impairment.* Retrieved from http://www.creating-joy.com/taskforce/tf_definitions.htm

American Counseling Association (ACA). (2014). American Counseling Association *2014 ACA code of ethics.* Retrieved from https://www.counseling.org/docs/default-source/ethics/2014-code-of-ethics.pdf?sfvrsn=2d58522c_4

American Mental Health Counselors Association (AMHCA). (2015). *AMHCA code of ethics.* Retrieved from http://www.amhca.org/HigherLogic/System/Download-DocumentFile.ashx?DocumentFileKey=5ff5bc94-e534-091e-c7c1-e3ea45cf943e&forceDialog=0

American Psychological Association (APA). (2017). *Ethical principles of psychologists and code of conduct.* Retrieved from https://www.apa.org/ethics/code/

American School Counselor Association (ASCA). (2016). *ASCA ethical standards for school counselors.* Retrieved from https://www.schoolcounselor.org/asca/media/asca/Ethics/EthicalStandards2016.pdf

Everall, R. D., & Paulson, B. L. (2004). Burnout and secondary traumatic stress: Impact on ethical behavior. *Canadian Journal of Counselling, 38*(1), 25–35.

Morse, G., Salyers, M. P., Rollins, A. L., Monroe-DeVita, M., & Pfahler, C. (2012). Burnout in mental health services: A review of the problem and its remediation. *Administration and Policy in Mental Health, 39*(5), 341–352. doi:org/10.1007/s10488-011-0352-1

National Association of Social Workers (NASW). (2017). *Code of ethics of the National Association of Social Workers (NASW).* Retrieved from https://www.socialworkers.org/About/Ethics/Code-of-Ethics/Code-of-Ethics-English

Sang Min, L., Seong Ho, C., Kissinger, D., & Ogle, N. T. (2010). A typology of burnout in professional counselors. *Journal of Counseling & Development, 88*(2), 131–138.

Sowa, C. J., & May, K. M. (1994). Occupational stress within the counseling profession: Implications for counselor training. *Counselor Education & Supervision, 34*(1), 19.

When Intervention Is Needed

What a day—it is only 8:30 a.m. and here are three students I need to see, a parent wanting an "immediate" phone call. I need to plan for my group this afternoon, and, oh yeah, I need to ... breathe!

—Jen, First-Year School Counselor

B reathing is something we do all the time, and you may not think we would have to instruct ourselves to do it explicitly. However, breathing, or taking a calming, deep breath, is one of the strategies that are readily available to help our well-being and is very impactful as a self-care technique. As you now are aware, it is not only essential to be cognizant of our well-being as counselors; it is an ethical standard that we are to follow. There are many ways to achieve and maintain a work and lifestyle of wellness and self-care, and as you read through the chapter, you are invited to reflect on what might work best for you in the short and long term. After reading this chapter, we are hoping you can complete the following:

a. Identify strategies you can do as an individual to maintain a healthy well-being.

b. Understand how you can manage the factors in the systems in which you work and live to be most effective.

c. Describe the strategies that can enhance your well-being by inviting others to join you on your journey as a counselor.

Life as a professional counselor has many rewards, such as helping and supporting others through difficult times and aiding clients' growth and development. However, as we have discussed, counselors are very much in danger of experiencing burnout and losing the ability to be effective both professionally and personally. The stress that can take a toll may be prevented or kept at bay by implementing strategies as an individual, by looking at the systems in which we live and by having the support of others. First, we will explore what you can do on an individual basis to implement strategies of self-care to achieve and maintain wellness.

What You Can Do (Self-Care and Self-Soothing)

Our time is limited and, as suggested in the following quote by author/poet Leo Christopher, *"there's only one thing more precious than our time, and that's who we spend it on."* Time is a precious resource and should be used wisely. As counselors, we are often focused on how to get everything we need to do completed within a tight time frame. Often, our time is truly not our own but rather dictated by the insurance contract, practice demands, school system, and a host of responsibilities in our work and personal lives.

If we take a minute to reflect on the quote ... wait, who has time to reflect? Exactly. We need to time take to reflect. Investing time in ourselves does not deter from all that we wish to do but rather enables us to do it more effectively. We need to use this precious research time wisely.

We are directed by our ethical codes to spend time engaging in our wellness and self-care as set forth by the ACA (2014, C. Introduction), the ASCA (2016, B.3.f.), the AMHCA (2015, C.h.), and the NASW (2017, 4.05.a.); we need to plan time for ourselves. Time to do what? The simple answer is to care for ourselves.

The World Health Organization (WHO) promotes self-care as encompassing several issues that include hygiene, nutrition, and lifestyle (WHO, 2014). These identified factors may serve as an excellent starting point for wellness and self-care.

Taking the time to take care of our physical and mental health provides a strong foundation for wellness. Strategies such as increased exercise and healthier eating have been found to reduce stress and promote wellness (Moore, Bledsoe, Perry, & Robinson, 2011). There is a plethora of information promoting a nutritional diet of healthy food and exercise (see https://www.healthline.com/health/fitness-exercise-eating-healthy as an example). Reframing the idea of maintaining a diet of nutritious foods and exercise as more than a "good" idea but as a prerequisite to competent, ethical professional practice may help counselors to take the need for developing and maintaining a healthy lifestyle seriously. Exercise 8.1 invites you to review the health of your lifestyle and the areas for which adjustment should be made.

EXERCISE 8.1

How Am I Doing?

Directions: Write down your typical diet and activity for a day or several days if your routine changes often. Use a resource, such as the following links, to see what type of diet and activity are recommended for someone of your age. You may want to talk to a colleague, friend, or both to hear more ideas about how to balance work, nutrition, and activity.

https://www.cdc.gov/healthyweight/calories/index.html
https://www.choosemyplate.gov/MyPlatePlan

How are you doing? It may not be easy to eat healthy meals and get regular exercise into your daily routine, and you may have to work at implementing these activities into your schedule. Likewise, you may need to intentionally plan to insert other fundamental and meaningful strategies for your well-being. Meditation and specifically mindfulness are certainly not new nor novel techniques employed to promote good mental health. However, they are strategies that have abundant research support, highlighting their value for maintaining the well-being of health-care providers (e.g., APA, 2012).

The use of breathing and mindfulness-based meditation has been proven to be useful for those with anxiety and other psychological illnesses (Nyklicek & Kuijpers, 2008), as well as helping to establish and maintain health and wellness (Baer, 2003) and preventing and reducing burnout (Epstein, 2003; Rothaupt & Morgan, 2007). Mindfulness meditation can promote mental acuity and awareness, decrease rumination, and enhance the capacity of attention and working memory (Corcoran, Farb, Anderson, & Segal, 2010) as by definition; it focuses one's attention to the present moment (Kabat-Zinn, 1994). The real beauty of intentionally paying attention to your breathing and refocusing if your mind wanders is that you can do this anywhere, any time of the day, as long as you remember to do it! There are numerous mindfulness programs to do for yourself and to share with clients and students, as well as apps to help get you started, such as this one: https://www.stopbreathethink.com/.

Given that counseling can be very demanding on one's emotional and mental well-being, counselors may also want to consider a spiritual path to holistic wellness (Cashwell, Bentley, & Bigbee, 2007). Mindfulness and spiritual practice often go hand in hand; thus, a spiritual path offers many opportunities for personal and professional healing and growth (Cashwell et al., 2007). See Case Illustration 8.1 for an example of a counselor who takes care of herself and uses strategies for wellness.

CASE ILLUSTRATION 8.1

A Mindful Counselor

Jocelyn has been a drug and alcohol counselor for more than 10 years. She works with three other counselors in a practice that is located in an urban setting. She works every afternoon and evening running groups and seeing individual clients. Her work is exhausting, as her clients are often court mandated and not cooperative, and many have been through traumatic experiences.

There are several counselor preparation programs near Jocelyn's practice, and she takes an intern every year. Her students are frequently heard remarking that Jocelyn does not seem phased by anything her clients say to her, and she always presents as calm and patient. Jocelyn makes sure that her student interns understand that the job is as demanding as it seems; however, she uses several strategies to help maintain physical and emotional wellness.

Jocelyn begins her day by getting up an hour before she needs to leave the house. She spends 15 minutes enjoying a cup of coffee and listening to her favorite music. She eats a breakfast that includes protein and fruit, packs a nutritious lunch, and makes her schedule for the day. Three days of the week she either takes a walk or cycles at the gym. The other two days, she does some yoga at home before she leaves.

Arriving at work two hours before her sessions begin, Jocelyn completes paperwork, such as forms for insurance, and then prepares for her sessions. All four counselors in the practice meet for scheduled group supervision 1 day a week and meet an additional day to go over other issues concerning the practice, which range from who is buying the coffee to who is maintaining the web page. They have all agreed to meet more often as needed. This schedule has proven to be useful for the past 5 years.

During the time that Jocelyn has her client sessions, she makes sure she takes at least 15 minutes between her clients and groups to jot down some quick notes and do a 1-minute mindful breathing exercise. She also schedules a 30-minute lunch break each day. Although she does not have time during the week for any social activities, she blocks out Saturday for social events. On Sundays, Jocelyn spends 2 hours at a community center that offers a nondenominational service that nourishes her spiritual well-being. She is sure to let her student interns know that even though she is very intentional and works hard at maintaining physical and mental wellness, there are times when she starts to feel overwhelmed, and during those times, she makes an appointment with her therapist. She feels she is a competent counselor in large part because of her being mindful of her physical and mental well-being.

Being intentional about taking care of your physical and mental well-being is vital for you personally and professionally. Making sure that you have strategies to maintain wellness in your daily life will go a long way to ensure your effectiveness as a counselor. Table 8.1 provides mindfulness-based interventions that are useful for those in training and practice.

Systemic Relief

Counseling can often be an isolating profession. Unlike many professions, counselors cannot merely share their day at work with friends and loved ones. As a counselor, you may feel as though you need to work alone in private to maintain confidentiality and the trust of your clients and students. This characteristic of professional practice not only reduces stress reduction outlets, such as sharing with friends, but also increases the felt level of singular, personal responsibility held by counselors and the stress that accompanies those responsibilities. However, this is not the only stress-contributing element for those in the role of counselor.

Counselors invest time and energy into their relationships and work with clients. There are factors, such as increasing caseloads, alternative work assignments, and even paperwork demands, that can interfere with a counselor's ability to provide all of the time he or she may desire to any one client. Also, if we add pressures from nonwork systems, such as family, and a counselor's desire to care for family members or maintaining friendships, it becomes clear that a counselor's well-being can be under siege

TABLE 8.1 Mindfulness-Based Interventions for Counselors

Target	Activity
Empathy	When engaging with a colleague or "practice" client, pause and reflect on what is happening within you. Attempt to identify internal responses. Ask the questions, "What is happening now?" "What am I feeling, and what might the other person be experiencing?"
Compassion	Practice sending a loving message to a loved one. Visualize this feeling toward a challenging client.
Counseling skills	In trainee dyads in roles of "counselor" and "client," let go of judgments and practice fully listening to the client. Pay attention to your internal experience in the presence of another, practicing to bring your attention back to the present when your mind wanders.
Decreased stress and anxiety	In dyads, track your internal feelings, thoughts, and sensations, attempting to focus on your experience of breathing. Practice with an accepting attitude toward internal reactions. Practice with another standing at varying distances with eyes open, eyes closed facing each other, and with backs facing each other. Pay attention to feelings of anxiety and fear.
Other	Practice formal sitting mindfulness meditation. In between sessions, take a minute to notice sensations of each breath and ask, "What is my experience right now?" Expand your awareness to your whole body with an attitude of acceptance.

Adapted from American Psychological Association (APA). (2012). What are the benefits of mindfulness? Retrieved from https://www.apa.org/monitor/2012/07-08/ce-corner

as a result of nonpersonal, systemic elements. Some of these environmental or system issues can be eased through addressing expectations and planned organization.

As we have noted, large caseloads and other demands of the job can and do take their toll on a counselor's well-being (Morse, Salyers, Rollins, Monroe-DeVita, & Pfahler, 2012; Sang Min, Seong, Kissinger, & Ogle, 2010; Sowa & May, 1994). School counselors report feelings of reduced effectiveness and emotional exhaustion, often stemming from having large caseloads and having to spend time on noncounseling duties (Bardhoshi, Schweinle, & Duncan, 2014). How do we deal with the responsibilities of our jobs when they become overwhelming? Case Illustration 8.2 describes some of the frustrations that may be felt when expectations are not clarified.

CASE ILLUSTRATION 8.2

I Thought That Was Your Job!

"Hey, Mike! Thanks for covering the art class until we found a sub. I didn't want to miss my prep period." Mike smiled and nodded and moved quickly to get back to his counseling office. He wanted to be a team player, but he didn't like missing his groups. It was bad enough that he had to spend so much time getting the test booklets ready for the state testing. Didn't anyone understand that his time could be so much better spent if he was seeing the students and not filling in when there was no substitute or filling in bubbles in test booklets? This isn't what he was trained to do and not what he wanted to spend his time doing as a school counselor!

Mike didn't want to make waves with the new principal, Jake. He was so hoping this principal would have made changes in how Mike was used, or misused, as Mike told the other counselors in his district. They had encouraged Mike to have a conversation with Jake, and so when he saw him that very afternoon in the hall, he timidly asked who was supposed to be fulfilling the role of the testing coordinator. Jake hadn't even stopped walking; he had just laughed and said, "I thought that was your job!"

As counselors, we are ready to advocate for our clients, and we must be ready to advocate for ourselves as well. Meeting with supervisors, administrators, and colleagues to review the expectations of the job, as well as task assignments, is an excellent place to begin. For example, in the school setting, principals often rely on the school counselor to oversee and engage in noncounseling tasks. Often, principals fail to have an understanding of how much time it takes to perform these noncounseling tasks and the opportunity costs accrued by having the counselor redirecting energy from the professional duties needed. The other problem is that often administrators do not fully understand or appreciate the professional level of training school counselors complete (Bardhoshi et al., 2014).

The ASCA (2019) provides guidelines in their national model for collaboration between the school counselor and principal, calling for an annual administrative conference to discuss and develop the counselor's goals for the year (ASCA, 2019). Clarifying expectations regarding caseload and duties can help make precious time more productive and effective. Using the ASCA (2019) guidelines as the rationale for reconfiguring the school counselor's role and function can provide the needed time and resources to attend to not only the remedial needs of the students but also to engage in those development programs so valuable to our student populations. Realigning job expectations could be the difference between having the time to facilitate small group counseling and coordinating mandated assessments.

In addition to gaining clarity over job expectations and ensuring that these are aligned to one's professional knowledge and skills, it is essential to craft a work environment—be that in a school or clinical setting—that fosters counselor ethical practice. Learning to set and maintain boundaries, providing informed consent, and clarifying issues of availability and criteria for termination, as well as scheduling time to manage paperwork, will help counselors maintain wellness and increase professional efficacy.

With a Little Help From a Friend

A counselor often works apart from other colleagues and spends much time interacting with clients or students. Although we have the charge of confidentiality, this does not mean that we should not talk with other professionals concerning questions regarding a client and most certainly regarding ourselves. Not only is it an effective and proven strategy to process something with another person (as a counselor, you most likely believe this to be true!), but it is ethically our job to do so. It is crucial to the self-care of a counselor to arrange regular supervision or consultation, regardless of the level of training or experience; establish a professional support network; and engage in systematic self-monitoring (Everall & Paulson, (2004).

In a counselor preparation program, you meet with your site supervisor, university instructor, and peers for supervision. In a school or clinical setting, you may have to reach out to other counselors and form your supervisory alliances. While being cognizant of confidential information, the use of an ethical decision-making model, including supervision, is appropriate and warranted. In addition, pursuing personal counseling for your well-being is part of our ethical standards and fully endorsed.

Using your professional contacts for supervision and personal counseling are a must for maintaining our professional competence and can help with maintaining wellness. Beyond those who offer professional support, friends, family, and others within our support systems, such as a church, clubs, or associations, can prove invaluable in facilitating the maintenance of our well-being. Of course, there are limits to what you should share with friends in regard to your work, but that does not mean you need to operate as if you are in black ops. You may certainly talk about work with a friend, making sure that there are no specifics given in the conversation, but it may prove much more beneficial to engage with friends and family around other valued, non-work-related issues and experiences. The old proverb, "All work and no play makes Jack a dull boy" can be very true. In the case of counselor well-being, we could add that it not only makes one a dull individual but also a potentially damaged one. So as a final directive, you are encouraged to "have some fun." Do not leave it to chance. Do not rely on the kindness and invitations of others. See having times of enjoyment, moments of a good belly laugh, or a time of genuinely connecting with a loved one as something worth planning for and scheduling. It is vital for your health, both personally and professionally!

A Takeaway

There are many ways a counselor can practice self-care, including following individual strategies for physical and mental well-being, collaborating with colleagues for a more efficient work environment and professional supervision, and being intentional with the activities in our personal lives. Thomas and Morris (2017) offer a seven-part model for creative self-care that includes the following:

1. Create a consistent plan to engage in mentally, emotionally, physically, and spiritually nourishing activities.
2. Schedule restorative rejuvenation when anticipating stress.
3. Prepare a list of emergency strategies for unanticipated stress.
4. Meet regularly with peers or colleagues for support.

5. Evaluate counselor-specific professional, perceptual, and personal challenges to self-care.

6. Record and review successes.

7. Include self-compassion as an essential element of healthy self-care.

The tools are here; the application is up to each of us.

KEYSTONES

- Counselors have an ethical responsibility to maintain physical and mental wellness.

- Counselors maintaining wellness are more effective in their personal and professional lives.

- There are strategies you can do individually that can help promote and maintain wellness. These include proper nutrition, exercise, and mindfulness techniques.

- Factors in your work and social systems can negatively impact your effectiveness as a counselor.

- Clarifying expectations, planning, and following ethical guidelines can help alleviate some of the factors that negatively impact effectiveness and well-being.

- Supervision and consultation with other professionals throughout your career as a counselor are ethical and expected.

- Schedule time to do something fun; it is important to your personal and professional well-being!

ADDITIONAL RESOURCES

In Print

Corey, G., Muratori, M., Austin, J. T., & Austin, J. A. (2018). *Counselor self-care.* Alexandria, VA: American Counseling Association.

Web Based

CDC https://www.cdc.gov/healthyweight/calories/index.html

Health https://www.health.com

Mindful.org https://www.mindful.org/

Mindspace http://www.meditationinschools.org/resources/

Positive Psychology/Mindfulness https://positivepsychology.com/mindfulnessmeditation/

REFERENCES

American Counseling Association (ACA). (2014). American Counseling Association *2014 ACA code of ethics*. Retrieved from https://www.counseling.org/docs/default-source/ethics/2014-code-of-ethics.pdf?sfvrsn=2d58522c_4

American Mental Health Counselors Association (AMHCA). (2015). *AMHCA code of ethics*. Retrieved from http://www.amhca.org/HigherLogic/System/DownloadDocumentFile.ashx?DocumentFileKey=5ff5bc94-e534-091e-c7c1-e3ea45cf943e&forceDialog=0

American Psychological Association (APA). (2012). *What are the benefits of mindfulness?* Retrieved from https://www.apa.org/monitor/2012/07-08/ce-corner

American School Counselor Association (ASCA). (2016). *ASCA ethical standards for school counselors*. Retrieved from https://www.schoolcounselor.org/asca/media/asca/Ethics/EthicalStandards2016.pdf

American School Counselor Association (ASCA). (2019). *The ASCA National Model: A framework for school counseling programs* (4th ed.). Alexandria, VA: Author.

Baer, R. (2003). Mindfulness training as a clinical intervention: A conceptual and empirical review. *Clinical Psychology: Science and Practice, 10*, 191–206.

Bardhoshi, G., Schweinle, A., & Duncan, K. (2014). Understanding the impact of school factors on school counselor burnout: A mixed-methods study. *The Professional Counselor, 4*(5), 426–443.

Cashwell, C. S., Bentley, D. P., & Bigbee, A. (2007). Spirituality and counselor wellness. *Journal of Humanistic Counseling, Education and Development, 46*(1), 66–81.

Corcoran, K. M., Farb, N., Anderson, A., & Segal, Z. V. (2010). Mindfulness and emotion regulation: Outcomes and possible mediating mechanisms. In A. M. Kring & D. M. Sloan (Eds.), *Emotion regulation and psychopathology: A transdiagnositc approach to etiology and treatment* (pp. 339–55). New York, NY: Guilford Press.

Epstein, R. M. (2003). Mindful practice in action (II): Cultivating habits of mind. *Families, Systems & Health, 21*, 11–17.

Everall, R. D. & Paulson, B. L. (2004). Burnout and secondary traumatic stress: Impact on ethical behaviour. *Canadian Journal of Counselling, 38*(1), 25–35.

Kabat-Zinn, J. (1994). *Wherever you go, there you are: Mindfulness meditation in everyday life*. New York, NY: Hyperion.

Moore, S.E., Bledsoe, L.K., Perry, A.R., & Robinson, M. A. (2011). Social work students and self-care: A model assignment for teaching. *Journal of Social Work Education, 47*(3), 545–553.

Morse, G., Salyers, M. P., Rollins, A. L., Monroe-DeVita, M., & Pfahler, C. (2012). Burnout in mental health services: A review of the problem and its remediation. *Administration and Policy in Mental Health, 39*(5), 341–352. doi:org/10.1007/s10488-011-0352-1

National Association of Social Workers (NASW). (2017). *Code of ethics of the National Association of Social Workers (NASW)*. Retrieved from https://www.socialworkers.org/About/Ethics/Code-of-Ethics/Code-of-Ethics-English

Nyklicek, I., & Kuijpers, K. F. (2008). Effects of mindfulness-based stress reduction intervention on psychological well-being and quality of life: Is increased mindfulness indeed the mechanism? *Annals of Behavioral Medicine, 35*(3) 331–340.

Rothaupt, J. W., & Morgan, M. M. (2007). Counselors' and counselor educators' practice of mindfulness: A qualitative inquiry. *Counseling and Values, 52,* 40–54.

Sang Min, L., Seong Ho, C., Kissinger, D., & Ogle, N. T. (2010). A typology of burnout in professional counselors. *Journal of Counseling & Development, 88*(2), 131–138.

Sowa, C. J., & May, K. M. (1994). Occupational stress within the counseling profession: Implications for counselor training. *Counselor Education & Supervision, 34*(1), 19.

Thomas, D. A., & Morris, M. H. (2017). Creative counselor self-care. *Ideas and Research You Can Use: VISTAS 2017.* Retrieved from https://www.counseling.org/knowledge-center/vistas/by-year2/vistas-2017/docs/default-source/vistas/creative-counselor-self-care

World Health Organization (WHO), Regional Office for South-East Asia. (2014). *Self care for health.* Retrieved from https://apps.who.int/iris/handle/10665/205887

Prevention Through Wellness Promotion

> *My mantra, "short-term pain for long-term gain," got me through*
> *graduate school, but I can't make this a daily occurrence!*
> *My self-care is always on the back burner!*
> *Something has got to give!*

—**Eugenia, High School Counselor**

The comment shared by a second-year high school counselor, Eugenia, might resonate with many new and seasoned counseling professionals. Given her life roles as a wife, a mother, a daughter, and a student, Eugenia was determined to get through her graduate school at all costs, even when those costs included her own mental and physical health.

Eugenia had very little time for herself, let alone the people in her life. Her mantra became an excuse for her lack of self-care. She reported that she engaged in little exercise or social life, with the hope that when she was done with graduate school, she would do better. Little did she know that the demands of a beginning professional had its own challenges and that something needed to change. The question is, what does it take to develop a wellness orientation? How do you as a current student or a beginning or seasoned professional develop a wellness mind-set, one that is practical and not just ideal?

After reading this chapter, the reader will be able to complete the following:

a. Describe the various dimensions of a wellness prevention model (physical, nutrition, social, and mental).

b. Develop a wellness prevention orientation that fits you as a person and a professional (wellness as an individual responsibility).

c. Describe systemic changes that can be implemented to facilitate wellness in the workforce (a systemic responsibility).

Wellness Prevention Model: Healthy Life Habits (From Nutrition and Exercise to Mindfulness)

Wellness is defined as "a sense that one is living in a manner that permits the experience of consistent, balanced growth in the physical, emotional, intellectual, social, and psychological dimension of human existence" (Adams, Bezner, Drabbs, Zambarano, & Steinhardt, 2000, p. 169). The first key phrase in this wellness definition that is noteworthy is "balanced growth."

Balance growth? How often do you (as a person or professional) make a New Year's resolution that includes some version of developing a healthy holistic lifestyle? The point is, most people know the value of creating balance in their health; however, doing so requires engaging in activities that might challenge your comfort level. Note, a healthy lifestyle does not necessarily equal the absence of disease. It does not mean that you will be immune to life's stress or emotional distress. A healthy lifestyle refers to the feeling of completeness and fulfillment in all aspects of a person's life.

Addressing wellness as a preventative measure requires a holistic approach with attention to the multifaceted parts of the human condition. Because human nature consists of biological, behavioral (psychological), and social conditions, Engel (1977) proposed the biopsychosocial approach as the model of care. Although Engel's model was specific to health-care delivery, the biopsychosocial approach to wellness is not unique, nor restricted, to health-care delivery systems. Engel's call to attend to physical, psychological, and social conditions of health have meaning and value to the management of a counselor's wellness. The integrated approach to wellness is similar to the "four legs of a table" analogy. A table is functional when all the legs are stable. When any of the legs breaks or is unstable, it renders the table ineffective. Similarly, counselors need to make a concerted effort to ensure *balance* in all aspects of their personal, as well as professional, lives.

Experiencing balance is but one aspect of wellness as defined by Adams et al. (2000). The second key aspect of the Adams et al. (2000) wellness definition to be considered is that living in balance needs to be experienced with consistency. Simply put, consistency requires counselors to attend to the whole self rather than sections of the self as part of their lifestyle. Consider the case of an elementary school counselor (see Case Illustration 9.1) who is "the" counselor responsible for the two elementary schools in her school district.

CASE ILLUSTRATION 9.1

How Do I Find Balance and Maintain Consistency?

Jennifer is a school counselor in a district where, because of financial constraints, school counselors are forced to work part time in more than one school. Jennifer is the school counselor for the only two elementary schools that are on opposite ends of the district's service area. Her commute from her house to each school is about 35 minutes. It takes her about 30 minutes to drive from one school to the other. As a result, she has structured her workweek to be present at both schools two-and-a-half days a week. Jennifer has a great relationship with the students, parents, administration, and staff at each of the schools. However, because of her split workweek, she feels stretched thin by the end of the week. She feels overwhelmed most days because she has to "catch up" with most of her caseload, which, by the way, is about 300 in each school. In each of the schools, there is a school psychologist, a social worker, school nurse, a school-based community counselor, and a visiting mental health consultant.

Jennifer is married with two children, one of whom has special needs. Her roles as a wife and a mother become her focus when she is not working. Sometimes, she becomes conflicted and challenged when either of her children is sick. As she puts it, "I have a full-time job as a school counselor and a full-time job as a mother." Her husband works about an hour away from their home. Her special needs child receives home services, which have become a lifesaver for Jennifer.

On most weekends, Jennifer spends time with her family and sometimes visits her parents who live about 20 minutes away from her home. She has two other siblings but both live out of state with their families. Therefore, she has power of attorney for her parents. Luckily, her parents are capable of caring for themselves. However, she goes to their home to help them with the budget and other needs. She is also an active member of her church, which means she spends half of her Sundays at church. Jennifer often finds herself running around during the day, and her only downtime is usually Saturday and Sunday evenings. She states, "I don't know how I do it, but I guess it's great to be young and energetic!"

Physical Dimension of Wellness (Physical Activity, Nutrition, Sleep, Screening)

In career-driven societies such as the United States, people often find themselves myopically focused on achievement and advancement. Such a narrow perspective and drive often come at the cost of attention to one's physical health and well-being. A recent report from the CDC (2019) indicates that 6 in 10 adults have chronic diseases, with 4 in 10 having two or more chronic diseases. While these statistics are alarming, what is perhaps more concerning is that the sources of these chronic diseases are often conditions that can be managed. Conditions contributing to numerous chronic conditions include obesity, cardiovascular heart disease, and diabetes, conditions that studies have shown can be associated with physical inactivity and unhealthy eating (Reiner, Niermann, Jekauc, & Woll, 2013; Warburton, Nicol, & Bredin, 2006).

The literature is unequivocal. Physical activity promotes general health, reduces the development of chronic illnesses (Reiner, et al., 2013; Warburton, et al., 2006), and increases endorphins that can promote overall mental health when associated with physical activities that are leisure oriented (White et al., 2017).

According to WHO (2019), adults need at least 150 minutes of moderately vigorous aerobic physical activity or at least 75 minutes of vigorous aerobic physical activity throughout the week. While numerous jobs and professions require physical activity, often strenuous, that is part of the performance of the job that elevates the individual's aerobic levels, counseling is not one of them. The sedentary nature of the counseling profession requires counselors to be intentional in incorporating physical activity into their daily routine. However, given the schedules, caseloads, and overall task demands encountered by those in the counseling profession, one might question the ability to incorporate physical activity into the daily routine consistently. While going to the gym and vigorously exercising is a form of healthy physical activity, so too are moderate physical activities such as lunchtime walks, after work walking or dancing and even energetically engaging with household chores.

In addition to exercise, a healthy lifestyle demands healthy eating. Healthy eating habits and "good nutrition is the bedrock of human well-being ... [which] enables optimal brain and immune system development and functioning" (Fanzo et al., 2015, p. 639). Ask any practicing counselor, "How many times have you worked through lunch?" You may be amazed at how commonplace it is for counselors to not only work through lunch but often ignore other bodily demands. Failure to attend to one's healthy eating can be exacerbated in settings such as a school, where counselors do not typically operate with a strict appointment schedule, are often requested to speak with teachers during "their" lunch, and may be surrounded by sweet snacks celebrating some faculty member's birthday.

Healthy eating does not equate with denial or even extreme restriction of those culinary temptations that are less than nutritious. Healthy eating implies a conscious effort in planning your daily eating patterns and the content of meals. "Cheating" is allowed, but it should be the exception to your style not the essence of your health habits. Thus using the food pyramid as your basis and staying within the recommended daily caloric intake (which is pegged at 2,000 for women and 2,500 for men) is an intentional way to attend to your physical well-being and maintain a healthy weight (NHS, 2016).

Another component of maintaining one's wellness is acquiring—again consistently—needed hours of restful sleep. Sleep is a critical component of one's physical wellness. However, the National Sleep Foundation (2019) reported that about 45% of Americans indicated poor or insufficient sleep. Not surprisingly, the same report indicated that about 67% of those with sleep issues generally have poor health conditions. In general, poor sleep patterns have the potential to affect the quality of life. Sleep problems can range "from a combination of acute or chronic problems with prolonged sleep onset latency (SOL), excessive wake after sleep onset (WASO), short total sleep time (TST), low sleep efficiency (SE), or poor sleep quality based on subjective and objective assessments" (Irish, Kline, Gunn, Buysse, & Hall, 2015, p. 24).

The number of those reporting poor or insufficient sleep and the expanse of the damage this may cause calls for the development of habits to foster and support healthy sleep. Iris and her colleagues (Irish, et al., 2015), following their review of empirical studies, recommended behavioral changes that may be helpful to some individuals but cautioned generalization: (a) reduce consumption of caffeine before bedtime, (b) reduce smoking and alcohol use, (c) avoid exercise close to bedtime, (d) engage in stress management and relaxation techniques, (e) limit noise, (f) practice regular sleep time, and (g) avoid daytime napping.

Psychological and Social (Connectedness) Dimensions of Wellness

In many ways, the counselor's "job" is one that is socially and psychologically isolating. Consider the work and the context in which that work is engaged. Counselors engage in highly emotional interactions that demand the counselor's full attention and experience of empathy, and the work is most often done in isolation of other coworkers or colleagues. The very nature of their work restricts counselors' opportunities to share successes or lament about their challenges or failures outside of the confines of their work environment. The intensity of the interactions they experience as part of their work and the professional requirement to hold the nature of those interactions in private can lead to social and emotional exhaustion. Given the isolating and draining nature of the work counselors do, it is critical that they engage in psychological and social preventative wellness activities.

One activity that is receiving much attention as a wellness-promoting activity for counselors is engagement in mindfulness practice (e.g., Campbell, Vance, & Dong, 2017; Epstein, 2003; Rothaupt & Morgan, 2007). Bishop et al. (2004) defined mindfulness as a two-component model, involving the "self-regulation of attention" and "a particular orientation towards one's experiences in the present moment ... that is characterized by curiosity, openness, and acceptance" (p. 232). Mindfulness requires the counselor to be present, being cognizant of the here and now, with the purpose of facilitating serenity.

Mindfulness can have affective, interpersonal, and intrapersonal benefits (Davis & Hayes, 2011). Mindfulness practices have been reported to prevent and reduce burnout (Epstein, 2003; Rothaupt & Morgan, 2007), thus enhancing counseling competency (Campbell et al., 2017) and fostering acceptance of one's challenging thoughts and feelings as opposed to encouraging one to alter or control them (Davis & Hayes, 2011). Affective benefits include emotional regulation, decreased reactivity, and increased response flexibility. Moreover, the intrapersonal benefits include the reduction of psychological distress, decreased stress and anxiety, increased self-efficacy, patience, intentionality, gratitude, and body awareness. When counselors feel good about themselves, it enhances interpersonal interactions. In addition, research has found that mental health providers have reported increased abilities in conceptualizing their clients' cases because of increased awareness of their experiences in therapy (Escuriex & Labbe, 2011).

Table 9.1 provides some activities that have been found to facilitate a counselor's ability to find and maintain a healthy lifestyle.

While understanding what one can do to achieve and maintain a healthy balance is essential, doing those things is what is needed. Exercise 9.1 invites you to begin "doing" by reflecting on your current state of healthy lifestyle practice.

TABLE 9.1   A Sample of Strategies for Establishing and Maintaining a Healthy Style

Intellectual Stimulation:
  * Attend professional development
  * Participate in professional discussion or peer supervision groups
  * Serve as a mentor
  * Learn a new skill unrelated to counseling (e.g., art class, cooking class)

Refocusing
  * Take time to remember positive work-related experiences
  * Maintain a journal documenting reminders of the value of your role and profession

Social Connection
  * Carve out time to engage with people who have similar interests, values, and experiences who can help reduce the psychological effects of stress
  * Engage in fun activities with family and friends over the weekend
  * Participate in weekly religious or spiritual practice (Coaston, 2017)

EXERCISE 9.1

Wellness Questionnaire

Directions: The following is a short survey to gauge your wellness. Please rate the following statements on a scale of 1–5: 1 = definitely, 2 = somewhat likely = 2, not certain = 3, somewhat unlikely = 4, definitely not = 5. Assess the areas that seem to be right on target and those in need of a change. Consider what you may do to implement that change. Also, consider consulting with a peer or supervisor regarding your needs.

1. I value my health, but I lack commitment to make changes.

   _____

2. I have a wellness plan. _____

3. My wellness plan includes physical activities. _____

4. I try to include physical activity every day. _____

5. My wellness plan includes paying attention to my nutrition.

   _____

6. I buy fruits and vegetables but don't eat them. _____

7. My wellness plans include paying attention to my psychological needs.

   _____

8. I engage in mindfulness activities on a daily basis. _____

9. My wellness plans include socialization with friends/family.

   _____

10. I have friends I hang out with during my free time. _____

11. I have no time to meet with my friends. _____

12. My job is my greatest source of stress. _____

13. I can take breaks at work, but I often do not. _____

14. My afternoon snacks are always healthy options. _____

15. My sleep hours range between 7 and 8 hours. _____

Developing a Wellness Orientation: An Ounce of Prevention Is Worth a Pound of Cure

At the beginning of this chapter, you were introduced to Eugenia, a second-year school counselor who seems to be hiding behind the mantra "short-term pain for long-term gain." Although this mantra served a purpose, she recognizes that she cannot continue to push her self-care needs under the rug, all in the name of enjoying them later. If Eugenia wants to make changes, how should she begin the process of building a wellness orientation that fits her current needs and future focus?

In this section, you will be introduced to the ABC model of personal wellness development.

A—Assess. This refers to the act of self-reflection and assessment of your total self! This is done by reflecting and reviewing your physical, psychological, and social wellness activities to ascertain where there is neglect. Remember, the goal is to create balance.

Questions to Consider When Assessing

- How much time do I devote to any form of physical activity?

- How is my meal planning?

- Do I eat a balanced diet?

- How is my stress level?

- How often do I engage in psychological or social activities?

- What is working well in all three domains?

- What is not working well?

- What goals can I make for my wellness in all three domains?

B—Build. Once you have identified the deficit area(s), you should then begin to build a plan to address the deficits. You may need to explore various options that fit your current role(s) in life. For instance, if you identify physical wellness as the area that needs the most improvement, you could examine your roles and identify the compromises you need to make to ensure that you are attending to your physical wellness. Make time for this; it is worth it! Be creative but realistic in your options. You may need to start small and then build on the plan(s). Several online resources have been provided in the web-based section to help you build your plans. You are unique, so explore several options that fit you.

C—Commit. This last section requires weighing your options and committing to the best plan. You may need to rely on your social support system to keep you accountable. Commitment to the selected options also implies reassessing after a specific period, preferably a month, to determine whether you are achieving your goals.

EXERCISE 9.2

Develop Your ABC Wellness Orientation

Directions: Using the ABC model, design a personal wellness orientation plan that fits you. In employing the ABC model, be as detailed and as specific as you can. It is okay to start small, so make the goals realistic and manageable.

Assess. Reflect on your physical, psychological, and social wellness activities. What one or two areas are you neglecting? Be specific.

Build. Begin to build a plan to address the deficits. Start small. Review the online resources provided in the web-based section of this chapter to help you build your plan.

Commit. It helps to share your desire and your plan with another as a way of making your commitment real. Review your plan after a month and determine if an adjustment should be made.

Systemic Changes: Fostering a Culture of Wellness in the Workplace

A system is as good as its members. When the workforce of a system is deficient, the system ceases to be functional; it becomes a system that is surviving, not thriving! Employers have a responsibility to create an environment that will nurture their employees' wellness. The composition of the human race is varied, and the demands of clients have changed, especially with increased globalization and diversity. Consequently, counselors' workload has increased, leading to a possible increase in emotional stress and burnout (Lambie, 2007; Sapolsky, 2004).

Lawson and Myers (2011) assessed professional counselors' quality of life, career-sustaining behaviors (CSBs), and wellness overall. Participants responded to questions related to their caseloads, their characteristics, and personal wellness practices. Results showed that the environment in which one works influences one's overall wellness. Counselors working in private practice settings, for example, reported higher wellness scores than those working in agencies or school settings. In addition, counselors with a smaller caseload of clients who have a history of trauma reported fewer feelings of burnout or compassion fatigue. Counselors in this study also identified their practice of self-care (including spending time with family; maintaining a sense of humor; balancing professional and personal lives, professional identity, and self-awareness; reflecting on positive experiences; and engaging in quiet leisure activities, among others) as being helpful to their CSB.

Most workers, including counselors, spend about one third of their day at the workplace, and when stress levels are not consciously mitigated, this can hinder productivity. Recently, there have been calls for a mental health day for the workforce. This is inspired by the increased reality that often employers do not make wellness of the workforce a priority. Some health-care organizations have implemented mindfulness-based stress reduction (MBSR) into their organizations. Belton (2018) reported that this might consist of 8-week classes and one final daylong retreat to teach meditation techniques to those who participate. Belton found that participants who engaged in these types of MBSR activities reported improved mood, increased calmness, greater satisfaction with their professional lives, and an increase in commitment and self-compassion. Other examples of institutional wellness programs can include cooking demonstrations, group fitness classes, wellness evaluations, coaching, massages, stress management, exercise equipment, and weight loss programs (Dabrh, Gorty, Jenkins, Murad, & Hensrud, 2016).

For counselors, research has demonstrated the value of supervision to the maintenance of their health and well-being (Bernard & Goodyear, 2014). Using the theoretical tenets of Bernard's (1997) discrimination model of supervision and a wellness undertone, Blount and Mullen (2015) proposed an integrated wellness model (IWM). The IWM suggests that supervisees engage in self-assessment to determine their levels of professional and personal wellness and "unwellness." With the help of their supervisors, they can, consequently, develop goals and action plans that can increase their wellness activities. Along with facilitating supervisees' awareness of their current wellness levels, supervisors can also help supervisees by discovering their awareness of how they influence their clients in their counseling sessions.

Integrative Care as Part of the Systemic Wellness Approach

Integrated care is a practice phenomenon that is gaining credence in the health sector because of its contribution to providing holistic, accessible, continuous, and cost-effective care to clients (Aguirre & Carrion, 2013; WHO, 2007). It posits that health care should be delivered from a more collaborative systemic practice where both the medical and mental health needs of a client are addressed using an interprofessional lens. While the focus is on improving health-care services for the client, such collaboration also holds great promise and benefits for the practitioners (Gersh, 2008; Glueck, 2015). The proximity or the easy communication established as a result of the team approach fosters consultation between the counselor and other professionals, thus reducing a counselors sense of "being alone" in such an important venture. This sense of support and connectedness is apparent in the reflections of one counselor addressing the complex needs of one client (see Case Illustration 9.2).

CASE ILLUSTRATION 9.2

If Only We Could Talk!

I've been working in a community mental health practice for well over 20 years, and I thought I saw it all. I didn't. It was late on a Friday evening, and I was finishing up my notes on my last client. Unexpectedly, I heard a knock at the office door, and when I opened, I found myself face-to-face with an individual who indeed would change my life.

Hashu was an 18-year-old female who presented with PTSD, having spent 3 years (14–17) as a victim of human trafficking and sex trafficking. My work with Hashu has left me with a sense of awe regarding the resiliency of the human spirit and a real sense of appreciation for the support and benefit (to self and client) of working in a collaborative setting.

Hashu's story was, at times, gut-wrenching. There were times in session when I think about one of my colleagues and silently say to myself, "If only we could talk." Feelings of a need to share with a colleague to seek advice, to find support, or to simply share the burden became a common occurrence while working with Hashu. Fortunately, I worked in a setting where support was available.

My work with Hashu invited—no make that demanded—collaboration with members of our legal team, medical staff, and social workers. Such collaboration not only added to the effective service provided to Hashu but also supported my own effectiveness and well-being.

KEYSTONES

- Wellness is living in a manner that permits consistent, balanced growth in the physical, emotional, intellectual, social, and psychological dimensions of life (Adams et al., 2000).

- Wellness needs to be approached in a holistic manner.

- To promote wellness, counselors should develop plans that integrate physical, psychological, and social activities.

- Wellness is a way of life, and to embrace it, a counselor can be proactive in assessing his or her lifestyle; building creative, practical options; and committing to the most realistic plan.

- Employers also have a responsibility to create an environment that will nurture the wellness of their employees because when the workforce of a system is deficient, the system becomes a surviving unit.

- Counselors can benefit from improved work schedules, sizable workload reduction, job clarity, communication flow, leadership support, and incentives.

- Integrated care can be a viable means of fostering wellness in the workforce. Counselors working in integrated care have suggested that it can be an effective model that promotes collaboration, team care approach, and interprofessional communication (Gersh, 2008; Glueck, 2015).

ADDITIONAL RESOURCES

In Print

Bernard, J. M., & Goodyear, R. K. (2014). *Fundamentals of clinical supervision* (5th ed.). Upper Saddle River, NJ: Pearson.

Corey, G., Muratori, M., Austin J. T., II, & Austin, J. A. (2018). *Counselor self care.* Alexandria, VA: American Counseling Association.

Sapolsky, R. M. (2004). *Why zebras don't get ulcers: An updated guide to stress, stress-related diseases, and coping.* New York, NY: W. H. Freeman.

Sockolov, M. (2018). *Practicing mindfulness.* Emeryville, CA: Althea Press.

Web Based

Online Resources for ABC Wellness Orientation:

https://www.integration.samhsa.gov/health-wellness/wellness-strategies/wellness.pdf

https://www.centre4activeliving.ca/media/filer_public/0c/d8/0cd87925-c9a7-4002-804c-199a119808a6/b-planning.pdf

https://www.cdc.gov/physicalactivity/basics/index.htm?CDC_AA_refVal=https%3A%2F%2Fwww.cdc.gov%2Fcancer%2Fdcpc%2Fprevention%2Fpolicies_practices%2Fphysical_activity%2Fguidelines.htm

https://www.wellspan.org/about-wellspan/wellspan-in-the-community/community-health-wellness/other-resources/activity-pyramid/

https://patient.info/healthy-living/physical-activity-for-health

https://www.quebec.ca/en/health/advice-and-prevention/healthy-lifestyle-habits/physical-activity/improving-your-health-through-physical-activity/

REFERENCES

Adams, T. B., Bezner, J. R., Drabbs, M. E. Zambarano, R. J., & Steinhardt, M. A. (2000). Conceptualization and measurement of the spiritual and psychological dimensions of wellness in a college population. *Journal of American College Health, 48*(4), 165–73.

Aguirre, J., & Carrion, V. G. (2013). Integrated behavioral health services: A collaborative care model for pediatric consumers in a low-income setting. *Clinical Pediatrics, 20*(10), 1–3.

Belton, S. (2018). Caring for the caregivers: making the case for mindfulness-based wellness programming to support nurses and prevent staff turnover. *Nursing Economics, 36*(4), 191–194.

Bernard, J. M. (1997). The discrimination model. In C. E. Watkins (Ed.), *Handbook of psychotherapy supervision* (pp. 310–327). New York, NY: Wiley.

Bernard, J. M., & Goodyear, R. K. (2014). *Fundamentals of clinical supervision* (5th ed.). Upper Saddle River, NJ: Pearson.

Bishop, S. R., Lau, M., Shapiro, S., Carlson, L., Anderson, N. D., Carmody, J. ... Devins, G. (2004). Mindfulness: A proposed operational definition. *Clinical Psychology: Science and Practice, 11*, 230–241.

Blount, A. J., & Mullen, P. R. (2015). Development of an integrative wellness model: Supervising counselors-in-training. *The Professional Counselor, 7*(1), 100–113.

Campbell, A., Vance, S. R., & Dong, S. (2017). Examining the relationship between mindfulness and multicultural counseling competencies in counselor trainees. *Mindfulness.* Advance online publication. doi:10.1007/s12671-017-0746-6

Center for Diseases Control and Prevention (CDC). (2019). Chronic diseases in America. Retrieved from https://www.cdc.gov/chronicdisease/resources/infographic/chronic-diseases.htm

Coaston, S. C. (2017). Self-care through self-compassion: A balm for burnout. *The Professional Counselor, 7*(3), 285–297.

Dabrh, A. M. A., Gorty, A., Jenkins, S. M., Murad, M. H., & Hensrud, D. D. (2016). Health habits of employees in a large medical center: Time trends and impact of a worksite wellness facility. *Scientific Reports, 6,* 1–7.

Davis, D. M., & Hayes, J. A. (2011). What are the benefits of mindfulness? A practice review of psychotherapy-related research. *American Psychological Association, 48*(2), 198–208.

Engel, G. L. (1977). The need for a new medical model: a challenge for biomedicine. *Science, 196*(4286), 129–136.

Epstein, R. M. (2003). Mindful practice in action (II): Cultivating habits of mind. *Families, Systems & Health, 21*, 11–17.

Escuriex, B. F., & Labbe, E. E. (2011). Health care providers' mindfulness and treatment outcomes: A critical review of the research literature. *Mindfulness, 2*(4), 242–253.

Fanzo, J. C., Graziose, M. M., Kraemer, K., Gillespie, S., Johnston, J. L., de Pee, S., ... West, K. P. (2015). Educating and training a workforce for nutrition in a post-2015 world. *Advanced Nutrition, 6*(6), 639–647. doi.org/10.3945/an.115.010041

Gersh, G. M. (2008). *Counselors working in integrated primary behavioral health and the influence of professional identity: A phenomenological study* (Doctoral dissertation). Retrieved from ProQuest Dissertations and Theses database. (UMI No. 3340183)

Glueck, B. P. (2015). Roles, attitudes, and training needs of behavioral health clinicians in integrated primary care. *Journal of Mental Health Counseling, 37*(5), 175–188.

Irish, L. A, Kline, C. E., Gunn, H. E., Buysse, D. J., & Hall, M. H. (2015). The role of sleep hygiene in promoting public health: A review of empirical evidence. *Sleep Medicine Reviews, 22*, 23–36. doi:10.1016/j.smrv.2014.10.001.

Lambie, G. W. (2007). The contribution of ego development level to burnout in school counselors: Implications for professional school counseling. *Journal of Counseling and Development, 85*, 82–88.

Lawson, G., & Myers, J. E. (2011). Wellness, professional quality of life, and career-sustaining behaviors: What keeps us well? *Journal of Counseling and Development, 89*, 163–171.

NHS. (2016). *What should my daily intake of calories be?* Retrieved from https://www.nhs.uk/common-health-questions/food-and-diet/what-should-my-daily-intake-of-calories-be/

National Sleep Foundation. (2019). Lack of sleep is affecting Americans, finds the National Sleep Foundation. Retrieved from https://www.sleepfoundation.org/press-release/lack-sleep-affecting-americans-finds-national-sleep-foundation

Reiner, M., Niermann, C., Jekauc, D., & Woll, A. (2013). Long-term health benefits of physical activity—a systematic review of longitudinal studies. *BMC Public Health, 13*(1), 813.

Rothaupt, J. W., & Morgan, M. M. (2007). Counselors' and counselor educators' practice of mindfulness: A qualitative inquiry. *Counseling and Values, 52*, 40–54.

Sapolsky, R. M. (2004). *Why zebras don't get ulcers: An updated guide to stress, stress-related diseases, and coping.* New York, NY: W. H. Freeman

Warburton, D., Nicol, C., & Bredin, S. (2006). Health benefits of physical activity: The evidence. *CMAJ: Canadian Medical Association Journal = Journal De L'Association Medicale Canadienne, 174*(6), 801–809.

White, R. L., Babic, M. J., Parker, P. D., Lubans, D. R., Astell-Burt, T., & Lonsdale, C. (2017). Domain-specific physical activity and mental health: A meta-analysis. *American Journal of Preventive Medicine, 52*(5), 653–666.

World Health Organization (WHO). (2007). Mental health and policy, planning, and service development. Retrieved from http://www.who.int/mental_health/policy/services/3_MHintoPHC_Infosheet.pdf

World Health Organization (WHO). (2019). Global strategy on diet, physical activity and health. Retrieved from https://www.who.int/dietphysicalactivity/factsheet_adults/en/

Resiliency: Key to Wellness

Truthfully, it has been one hell of a month. The number of clients I have encountered who survived significant life crises and trauma is overwhelming. There are times when I just don't think I can hear another story of trauma. I have never seen anything like it. However, I guess anything that doesn't kill you will make you stronger.

—Jorge, Domestic Abuse Counselor

"**A**nything that doesn't kill you can make you stronger." Jorge's perspective on what appears to have been a very stressful month of work is reflective of a counselor with resilience. A counselor who is resilient can respond to adversity with growth and a relatively positive outcome (Rutter, 2007; Saleebey, 2006).

Resilience can not only serve as a foundation for assisting counselors in dealing with stress but also as the preservation of service standards. Resilience is an essential factor in the creation and maintenance of a counselor's personal and professional well-being. Understanding the nature of resiliency and the factors that contribute to the development of counselor resiliency serves as the focus of this chapter.

After reading this chapter, the reader will be able to complete the following:

a. Describe the characteristics of resiliency.

b. Explain the factors, both individual and organizational, that contribute to the development of resiliency.

c. Assess the current state of resiliency.

Resiliency

An attempt to define resiliency is challenging in that there is no one commonly held definition of resiliency (McGeary, 2011). Most agree that resiliency reflects an individual's capacity to overcome adversities that would otherwise have been expected to result in negative consequences (Gito, Ihara, & Ogata, 2013). It is "the ability to bounce back from adversity, persevere through difficult times, and return to a state of internal equilibrium" (Edward, 2005, p. 143).

Resilience entails the interaction of neurobiological and psychosocial factors that facilitate coping with stress and adversity while preserving normal physical and psychological functioning that may result in thriving or flourishing (Elisei, Sciarma, Verdolini, & Anastasi, 2013). It is "a dynamic process wherein individuals display positive adaptation despite experiences of significant adversity or trauma" (Luthar & Cicchetti, 2000, p. 858).

Factors Associated With Resiliency

As a concept, resilience has been identified as a complex phenomenon that focuses on protective factors that contribute to positive outcomes despite the presence of risk and seemingly devastating disadvantages in life (Dent & Cameron, 2003; Mancini & Bonanno, 2006).

Resilience was initially understood to be a personality trait or the result of a number of personal factors (Fayombo, 2010; Lam & McBride-Chang, 2007). More recently, the concept was redefined to include the effect of organizational context (Beddoe, Davys, & Adamson, 2011; Earvolino-Ramirez, 2007). Extensive clinical research has established that both external (contextual) and internal (psychological) characteristics influence one's capacity for resilience (Luthar, Cicchetti, & Becker, 2000; Masten, Best, & Garmezy, 1990).

Personal Factors

Psychological resilience involves cognitive, emotional, social, and physical skills.

Resiliency has been associated with emotional and social competencies (Kinman & Grant 2011), positive emotions, optimism, and hope (Collins, 2008; Koenig & Spano, 2007; Tugade & Fredrikson, 2004), as well as hardiness and stress-resistant qualities (Beddoe et al., 2011).

Cognitive Skills and Orientation

Cognitive skills that build resiliency include learning how to identify and dispute negative thinking, thinking optimistically, and reframing thoughts or ideas into proactive ones. Using critical thinking strategies to make more effective and accurate appraisals of negative events and engaging effective coping and problem-solving skills has been associated with the presence of resilience (Wilks & Spivey, 2010).

In terms of cognitive orientation or perspective, a resilient practitioner maintains a sense of meaningfulness even in the face of challenging experiences and uses past successes to overcome current challenges (Connor, 2006). Resilient individuals find meaning in adversity; this meaning-making tends to facilitate personal growth and a renewed sense of and gratitude for life. Adults who can look to the future and not focus on the past seem to fare best. Or, as Donald Meichenbaum (2012) suggests, resilient individuals approach life and life's challenges with flexible thinking and an optimistic view.

Emotional Intelligence

Emotional intelligence is another trait or skill that buffers stressors and builds resilience. Emotional intelligence skills include self-awareness, other awareness, and modulation of emotions, as well as identifying emotions in others and responding appropriately and effectively in a positive manner.

Interpersonal Skills and Connections

A primary factor in resilience is having caring and supportive relationships. Strong interpersonal skills help buffer stress and encourage support from others. Experiencing trusting, loving relationships that provide encouragement and reassurance can bolster an individual's resilience (APA, 2014).

Behavioral

Those who maintain resilience take action when crises occur while seeing adversity as part of life. They feel competent to solve problems, nurture and care for themselves to stay healthy, manage their emotions, and have a realistic sense of hardship.

Organizational/Practice Factors

In addition to individual, personal factors found to contribute to the development and maintenance of resilience, a number of organizational and practice factors have also been found to be associated with the presence of resilience. Horwitz (1998), for example, outlined four principles aimed at promoting resilience in social work practice. The principles identified included (1) minimizing exposure to trauma, (2) avoiding negative chain reactions after exposure to a traumatic experience, (3) developing self-esteem by way of gaining opportunities to achieve goals in an environment that is both supportive and validating, and (4) being open to new opportunities so as to uphold a positive view of the future as a counterbalance to the negative aspects of their work.

Finding Balance

Those exhibiting resilience are committed to achieving "a balance between occupational stressors and life challenges while fostering professional values and career sustainability" (Fink-Samnick, 2009, p. 331). Managing personal and professional boundaries and work-life balance are not only associated with resilience but also promote subjective well-being and longevity in the profession (Graham & Shier, 2010; Lewis & Rajan-Rankin, 2013).

Developing Resiliency

Resiliency undoubtedly contributes to a counselor's ability to not only overcome stressors but also find personal meaning in them (Grant & Kinman, 2012, p. 1). Counselors with high levels of resilience exhibited faster physiological and emotional recovery from stressful life events (i.e., heavy caseloads and stressful work conditions; Ong, Bergeman, Bisconti, & Wallance, 2006.). Building resilience can assist the professional counselor with negotiating the challenging and demanding work environment of the mental health care field, reducing the risk of ethical mistakes, and increasing the sense of purpose and mission for the counselor.

Given that resilience is a protective factor engendering well-being (Bonnano, 2004; Grant & Kinman, 2012) and a "buffer" that protects individuals from adverse environmental influences and forces (Jackson, Firtko, & Edenborough, 2007), it would appear that it is beneficial for counselors to focus on cultivating and building their own resilience (Osborn, 2004).

While resiliency may be dispositional and trait-like, it is not a trait that people either have or do not have. There is considerable evidence that it is state-like and open to development (e.g., Coutu, 2002; Maddi & Koshaba, 1984; Reivich & Shatte, 2002).

Self-Assessment

Lawson and Venart (n.d.) reporting on the ACA's task force on impaired counselors noted, "One of the most important skills counselors can learn in guarding against impairment is the regular practice of self-monitoring and self-care activities" (p. 244). Developing one's resilience begins with the assessment of current levels of resilience.

One useful tool for monitoring one's level of resilience was created by Al Siebert, the founder of the Resilience Center in Portland. The instrument, "How Resilient Are You" is found in Exercise 10.1. Employment of this measure provides a snapshot of one's current level of resiliency.

EXERCISE 10.1

How Resilient Are You?

Directions: Rate yourself from 1 to 5 (1 = strongly disagree; 5 = strongly agree):

- I'm usually optimistic. I see difficulties as temporary and expect to overcome them.

- Feelings of anger, loss, and discouragement don't last long.

- I can tolerate high levels of ambiguity and uncertainty about situations.

- I adapt quickly to new developments. I'm curious. I ask questions.

- I'm playful. I find the humor in rough situations and can laugh at myself.

- I learn valuable lessons from my experiences and the experiences of others.

- I'm good at solving problems. I'm good at making things work well.

- I'm strong and durable. I hold up well during tough times.

- I've converted misfortune into good luck and found benefits in bad experiences.

Interpretation

Less than 20: Low Resilience. You may have trouble handling pressure or setbacks and may feel deeply hurt by any criticism. When things don't go well, you may feel helpless and without hope. Consider seeking professional counsel or support in developing your resiliency skills. Connect with others who share your developmental goals.

20–30: Some Resilience. You have some valuable pro-resiliency skills but also plenty of room for improvement. Strive to strengthen the characteristics you already have and to cultivate the characteristics you lack. You may also wish to seek some outside coaching or support.

30–35: Adequate Resilience. You are a self-motivated learner who recovers well from most challenges. Learning more about resilience and consciously building your resiliency skills will empower you to find more joy in life, even in the face of adversity.

35–45: Highly Resilient. You bounce back well from life's setbacks and can thrive even under pressure. You could be of service to others who are trying to cope better with adversity.

Taken from: Siebert, A. (2005). Resiliency Quiz—How Resilient are you? http://www.resiliencyquiz.com/index.shtml

An additional process found useful in the identification of a counselor's current level of resiliency and the establishment of a healthy balance in life is the Pie of Life Exercise (Nugent, 2004). Exercise 10.2 invites you to engage in this self-monitoring technique.

EXERCISE 10.2

Pie of Life Exercise

Directions:

1. On a blank piece of paper, draw a large circle to represent your life.

2. Place a smaller circle in the center to represent you and label it with your name.

3. Thinking of your life as a pie, divide the slices and label them to show the various activities that you are engaged in on a regular basis. Some

examples of potential "pie slices" are work, learning, family and other relationships, contributions to others, fun and leisure, physical and emotional self-care, and spiritual well-being.

4. Reflect on your current life by considering the following questions, and share your responses with a partner:

   · Am I living a balanced life?

   · Are my priorities and values reflected in this allocation of time?

   · If I had one month left to live, is this the way I would allocate my time?

   · Am I involved in too many activities?

   · How much of my time is spent caring for others? For myself?

   · Are there areas of my life that need my attention?

   · Is there a dream or desire that keeps getting put on the back burner that I'd like to focus on now?

   · What needs less attention? More attention?

   · What changes do I want to make?

   · What is one commitment I can now make to change the balance toward what I want for my life?

Source: Nugent, C. (2004). *Replenish the well: An experience in self-care, workshop presented at peer services: A life in the community for everyone*. Fifth Annual Conference of the Substance Abuse and Mental Health Services Administration, Center for Substance Abuse Treatment's Recovery Community Services Program, Washington, DC.

Taking Action

Building resilience does not happen by chance (Lawson & Myers, 2011); instead, it is based on the active practice of decisions that lead to wellness and health. There are multiple methods for building resiliency—for example, altering levels of risk (Masten, 2001), fostering self-enhancement (Taylor & Brown, 1988), and using positive emotions (Tugade & Frerickson, 2004). Positive emotions, which may take the form of laughter or smiles, may be vital toward building resiliency (Bonanno, Noll, Putnam, O'Neill, & Tickett, 2003). Skovholt (2001) reported that in a study about coping strategies used by psychotherapists, 82% endorsed having a sense of humor as a "career sustaining behavior" (p. 151).

In addition, it has been suggested that activities that yield a sense of satisfaction from working with clients are key to resisting threats, such as compassion fatigue, burnout, and secondary traumatization (Lawson & Myers, 2011). It has been suggested that counselors intentionally work on building specific CSBs—that is, "personal and professional activities … to extend, enhance, and more fully enjoy their work experiences" (Lawson & Myers, 2011, p. 165)—into their daily lives as a step toward maintaining wellness.

Given that the work that counselors do can be characterized as one of "people intensity" (Skovholt, 2001, p. 160), silence, as an experience of solitude and connection with the transcendent, can be refreshing and rejuvenating (Skovholt, 2001). Regardless of a person's spiritual or religious worldview, it is the cultivation of sacred moments—that is, "a moment in time imbued with sacred qualities" (Goldstein, 2007, p. 1002)—that can be restorative. Identifying that which is "sacred" is undoubtedly unique to each individual. The commonality, regardless if it occurs while looking at a countryside, seeing a sunrise, or more formally engaging in prayer or meditation, is that a sacred moment provides one with an opportunity to transcend beyond herself or himself and provides a connection with others. Gaining a larger perspective can reignite a sense of purpose and meaning in life, which in turn can offer hope and reduce stress (Goldstein, 2007). This was certainly true for one licensed professional counselor (see Case Illustration 10.1).

CASE ILLUSTRATION 10.1

Simple Steps to Big Results

The story was shared by a 48-year-old licensed professional counselor with multiple advanced degrees and certifications whom we will call Joseph. Joseph had a very successful and thriving clinical practice. His practice grew from what was once a part-time practice to one now engaging in over 35 hours of direct clinical contact each week, including supervising three additional practitioners. The exhaustion factor, as one might suspect, was high.

Joseph noted that he began to recognize signals that he was starting to experience burnout. He found himself emotionally disengaged, not only from his family and friends but also from clients and the practitioners he supervised. While no one within his practice nor his circle of family and friends noticed or said anything, he was very clear that his level of job and life satisfaction were on the wane.

Taking the directive of "doctor, heal thy self," he contracted for some short-term therapeutic support. In the process, it became increasingly clear that his work life and personal life were completely out of balance. He noted that he very rarely engaged in the golf, biking, or hiking activities that he truly loved. He somewhat embarrassingly confessed that it had been over a year since he went to see any of his daughter's volleyball games or attended his son's band performances. He stated that he was simply too exhausted, too physically and psychologically "spent" to do anything else after work.

While a number of suggestions geared toward regaining a healthy life balance were discussed, the one that seemed the simplest to employ and that had almost immediate positive effects was his decision to build in "quiet moments" throughout his day. Given his heavy caseload, it was not reasonable to take large blocks of time for meditation or reflection during the workday. What he did do, however, was to commit to sticking to a 50-minute hour, wherein he used the time between sessions to practice relaxation exercises, including breathing and imagery. In addition, a couple of his clients liked to "walk and talk" at his professional campus, and the nature of their work together permitted moving sessions out of the office to enjoy the surroundings.

These simple steps of taking moments of calm and reflection, along with reengaging with walking carried over to his home life where he not only set aside time for daily meditation but also regularly walked with his wife and/or the children following dinner. The process, while somewhat simplistic, was extremely beneficial in terms of encouraging the institution of other healthy, life-balancing activities and curtailing the downward spiral experienced by this clinician.

Sometimes, as evident in Case Illustration 10.1, the intervention, while powerful, is anything but complex or dramatic. Along this same line, Harker, Pidgeon, Klaassen, and King (2016) suggest that a factor that can contribute to the development of resilience is the practice of mindfulness. Increased levels of mindfulness have been reported to be associated with improvement in distress tolerance (Feldman, Dunn, Stemke, Bell, Greeson, 2014), emotion regulation skills (Lutz et al., 2014), and psychological flexibility (Masuda & Tully, 2012). Increased mindfulness has been shown to be correlated positively to psychological well-being and negatively associated with burnout and secondary traumatic stress (Mackenzie, Poulin, & Seidman-Carlson, 2006; Thieleman & Cacciatore, 2014).

With respect to one's work and working conditions, Osborn (2004) suggested that counselors need to (1) be selective and intentional, (2) be aware of time restrictions, (3) be accountable, and (4) be conservative with resources of skill and energy as part of enhancing stamina. This may involve counselors learning to say "no" and setting limits on what it is they choose to engage.

Numerous strategies have been suggested as helpful for the development and maintenance of counselors' resiliency. A list of 10 such strategies was developed by the APA and are provided in Table 10.1 as one final guide to the development and maintenance of your level of resiliency.

KEYSTONES

- Resiliency is "the ability to bounce back from adversity, persevere through difficult times, and return to a state of internal equilibrium" (Edward, 2005, p. 143).

- Resilience entails the interaction of neurobiological and psychosocial factors that facilitate coping with stress and adversity while preserving normal physical and psychological functioning that may result in thriving or flourishing.

- Extensive clinical research has established that both external (contextual) and internal (psychological) characteristics influence one's capacity for resilience.

- Psychological resilience involves cognitive, emotional, social, and physical skills, such as emotional and social competencies, positive emotions, optimism and hope, and hardiness and stress-resistant qualities.

TABLE 10.1   Ten Ways to Build Resilience

Make connections. Good relationships with close family members, friends, or others are important. Accepting help and support from those who care about you and will listen to you strengthens resilience. Some people find that being active in civic groups, faith-based organizations, or other local groups provides social support and can help with reclaiming hope. Assisting others in their time of need can also benefit the helper.

Avoid seeing crises as insurmountable problems. You can't change the fact that highly stressful events happen, but you can change how you interpret and respond to these events. Try looking beyond the present to how future circumstances may be a little better. Note any subtle ways in which you might already feel somewhat better as you deal with difficult situations.

Accept that change is a part of living. Certain goals may no longer be attainable as a result of adverse situations. Accepting circumstances that cannot be changed can help you focus on circumstances that you can alter.

Move toward your goals. Develop some realistic goals. Do something regularly, even if it seems like a small accomplishment, that enables you to move toward your goals. Instead of focusing on tasks that seem unachievable, ask yourself, "What's one thing I know I can accomplish today that will help me move in the direction I want to go?"

Take decisive actions. Act on adverse situations as much as you can. Take decisive actions rather than detaching completely from problems and stresses and wishing they would just go away.

Look for opportunities for self-discovery. People often learn something about themselves and may find that they have grown in some respect as a result of their struggle with loss. Many people who have experienced tragedies and hardship have reported better relationships, greater sense of strength even while feeling vulnerable, increased sense of self-worth, more developed spirituality, and heightened appreciation for life.

Nurture a positive view of yourself. Developing confidence in your ability to solve problems and trusting your instincts helps build resilience.

Keep things in perspective. Even when facing very painful events, try to consider the stressful situation in a broader context and keep a long-term perspective. Avoid blowing the event out of proportion.

Maintain a hopeful outlook. An optimistic outlook enables you to expect that good things will happen in your life. Try visualizing what you want rather than worrying about what you fear.

Take care of yourself. Pay attention to your own needs and feelings. Engage in activities that you enjoy and find relaxing. Exercise regularly. Taking care of yourself helps to keep your mind and body primed to deal with situations that require resilience.

Additional ways of strengthening resilience may be helpful. For example, some people write about their deepest thoughts and feelings related to trauma or other stressful events in their lives. Meditation and spiritual practices help some people build connections and restore hope.

> While resiliency may be dispositional and trait-like, it is not a trait that people either have or do not have. There is considerable evidence that it is open to development.

- Developing one's resilience begins with the assessment of current levels of resilience. There are numerous instruments to assist in such self-assessment.

- Methods or strategies for building resiliency include altering levels of risk, fostering self-enhancement, using positive emotions, and engaging in ways of connecting with the transcendent (e.g., use of silence and solitude, mindfulness, engaging in spiritual moments).

ADDITIONAL RESOURCES

In Print

Hernandez, P., Gangsei, D., & Engstrom, D. (2007). Vicarious resilience: A new concept in work with those who survive. *Family Process, 46*(2), 229–241.

Parry, S. (Ed.) (2017). *Effective self-care and resilience in clinical practice: Dealing with stress, compassion fatigue and burnout.* London, UK: Jessica Kingsley Publishers.

Saakvitne, K. W., Pearlman, L. A., & the Staff of the Traumatic Stress Institute. (1996). *Transforming the pain: A workbook on vicarious traumatization.* New York, NY: W.W. Norton.

Wicks, R. (2010). *Bounce: Living the resilient life.* New York, NY: Oxford University Press.

Web Based

APA: The Road to Resilience. https://www.apa.org/helpcenter/road-resilience.aspx

ASHP Consulting Services: Clinician Well-Being Knowledge Hub. https://www.ashp.org/Pharmacy.../Resource.../Clinician-Well-Being-and-Resilience

The Trauma Research, Education, and Training Institute, Inc.: Provides information and training to increase the abilities of mental health and social service workers to provide effective, ethical treatment for survivors of traumatic life experiences. http://ww3.treati.org/

REFERENCES

American Psychological Association (APA). (2014). The road to resilience. Retrieved from https://studentsuccess.unc.edu/files/2015/08/The-Road-to-Resiliency.pdf

Beddoe, L., Davys, A., and Adamson, C., (2011). Educating resilient practitioners. *Social Work Education, 32*(1), 100–117.

Bonnano, G. (2004). Loss, trauma and human resilience: Have we underestimated the human capacity to thrive after extremely adverse events, *American Psychologist, 59*(1), pp. 20–8.

Bonanno, G. A., Noll, J. G., Putnam, F. W., O'Neill, M., & Tickett, P. (2003). Predicting the willingness to disclose childhood sexual abuse from measures of repressive coping and dissociative experiences. *Child Maltreatment, 8*, 1–17.

Collins, S. (2008). Social workers, resilience, positive emotions and optimism. *Practice: Social Work in Action, 19*(4), 255–269.

Connor, K. M. (2006). Assessment of resilience in the aftermath of trauma. *Journal of Clinical Psychiatry, 67*(Suppl.2), 46–49.

Coutu, D. L. (2002). How resilience works. *Harvard Business Review, 80*(2), 46–55.

Dent, R. J., & Cameron, R.J.S. (2003). Developing resilience in children who are in public care: The educational psychology perspective. *Educational Psychology in Practice, 19*(1), 3–17.

Edward, K. (2005). The phenomenon of resilience in crisis care mental health clinicians. *International Journal of Mental Health Nursing, 14*(2), 142–148.

Earvolino-Ramirez, M. (2007). Resilience: A concept analysis. *Nursing Forum, 42*(2), 73–82.

Elisei, S., Sciarma, T., Verdolini, N., & Anastasi, S. (2013). Resilience and depressive disorders. *Psychiatria Danubina, 2*, 263–267.

Fayombo, G. A. (2010). The relationship between personality traits and psychological resilience among the Caribbean adolescents. *International Journal of Psychological Studies, 2*(2), 105–116.

Feldman, G., Dunn, E., Stemke, C., Bell, K., & Greeson, J. (2014). Mindfulness and rumination as predictors of persistence with a distress tolerance task. *Personality and Individual Differences, 56*, 154–158.

Fink-Samnick, E. (2009). The professional resilience paradigm: Defining the next dimension of professional self-care. *Professional Case Management, 14*(6), 330–332. doi: 10.1097/NCM.0b013e3181c3d483.

Gito, M., Ihara, H., & Ogata, H. (2013). The relationship of resilience, hardiness, depression and burnout among Japanese psychiatric hospital nurses. *Journal of Nursing Education and Practice, 3*(11), 12–18.

Goldstein, E. D. (2007). Sacred moments: Implications on well-being and stress. *Journal of Clinical Psychology, 63*, 1001–1019

Graham, R. J., & Shier, M. L. (2010.) The social work profession and subjective well-being: The impact of a profession on overall subjective well-being. *British Journal of Social Work, 40*(5), 1553–1572.

Grant, L., & Kinman, G. (2012). Enhancing well-being in social work students: Building resilience for the next generation. *Social Work Education, 31*(5), 605–621.

Harker, R., Pidgeon, A. M., Klaassen, F., & King, S. (2016). Exploring resilience and mindfulness as preventative factors for psychological distress burnout and secondary traumatic stress among human service professionals. *Journal of Prevention, Assessment & Rehabilitation, 54*(3), 631–637.

Horwitz, M. (1998). Social worker trauma: Building resilience in child protection social workers. *Smith College Studies in Social Work, 68*(3), 363–377.

Jackson, D., Firtko, A., & Edenborough, M. (2007). Personal resilience as a strategy for surviving and thriving in the face of workplace adversity: A literature review. *Journal of Advanced Nursing, 60*(1), 1–9.

Kinman, G., & Grant, L. (2011). Exploring stress resilience in trainee social workers: The role of social and emotional competencies. *British Journal of Social Work, 41*(2), 261–275.

Koenig, T., & Spano, R. (2007). The cultivation of social workers' hope in personal life and professional practice. *Journal of Religion and Spirituality in Social Work, 26*(3), 45–61.

Lam, C. B., & McBride-Chang, C. A. (2007). Resilience in young adulthood: The moderating influences of gender-related personality traits and coping flexibility. *Sex Roles, 56*(3), 150–172.

Lawson, G., & Venart, B. (n.d.). Preventing counselor impairment: Vulnerability, wellness, and Resilience. American Counseling Association Vista Online. Retrieved from https://www.counseling.org/Resources/Library/VISTAS/vistas05/Vistas05.art53.pdf

Lawson, G., & Myers, J. E. (2011). Wellness, professional quality of life, and career sustaining behaviors: What keeps us well? *Journal of Counseling & Development, 89,* 163–171.

Lewis, S., & Rajan-Rankin, S. (2013). Deconstructing "family supportive cultures": A vision for the future. In S. A. Y. Poelmans, J. Greenhaus, & M. L. H. Maestro (Eds.), *Expanding the boundaries of work-family research: A vision for the future* (pp. 53–69). London, UK: Palgrave MacMillan.

Luthar, S. S., & Cicchetti, D. (2000). The construct of resilience: Implications for interventions and social policies. *Development and Psychopathology, 12*(4), 857–885.

Luthar, S. S., Cicchetti, D., & Becker, B. (2000). The construct of resilience: A critical evaluation and guidelines for future work. *Child Development, 71*(3), 543–562.

Lutz, J., Herwig, U., Opialla, S., Hittmeyer, A., Jancke, L., Rufer, M., Grosse, H. M., & Bruhl A. B. (2014). Mindfulness and emotion regulation—an fMRI Study. *Social Cognitive and Affective Neuroscience, 9*(6), 776–785.

Mackenzie, C. S., Poulin, P. A. & Seidman-Carlson, R. (2006). A brief mindfulness-based stress reduction intervention for nurses and nurse aides. *Applied Nursing Research, 19,* 105.

Maddi, S. R., & Koshaba, D. M. (1984). *Resilience at work: How to succeed no matter what life throws at you.* New York, NY: AMACO.

Mancini, A. D., & Bonanno, G. A. (2006). Resilience in the face of potential trauma: Clinical practices and illustrations. *Journal of Clinical Psychology, 62*(8), 971–985.

Masten, A. S. (2001). Ordinary magic: Resilience processes in development. *American Psychologist, 56*(3), 227–238.

Masten, A. S., Best, K. M., & Garmezy, N. (1990). Resilience and development: Contributions from the study of children who overcome adversity. *Development and Psychopathology, 2*(4), 425–444.

Masuda, A., & Tully, E. C. (2012). The role of mindfulness and psychological flexibility in somatization, depression, anxiety, and general psychological distress in a non-clinical college sample. *Journal of Evidence-Based Complementary & Alternative Medicine, 17*(1), 66–71.

McGeary, D. (2011). Making sense of resilience. *Military Medicine, 176*(6), 603–604.

Meichenbaum, D., (2012). *Roadmap to resilience: A guide for military, trauma victims and their families.* Clearwater, FL: Institute Press.

Nugent, C. D. (2004). Replenish the well: An experience in self-care. Workshop presented at 5th Annual Conference of Substance Abuse and Mental Health Services Administration, Washington, DC. Retrieved from http://www.counseling.org/wellness_taskforce/index.htm

Ong, A. D., Bergeman, C. S., Bisconti, T. L., & Wallance, K. A. (2006). Psychological resilience, positive emotions, and successful adaption to stress in later life. *Journal of Personality and Social Psychology, 91*(4), 730–749.

Osborn, C. J. (2004). Seven salutary suggestions for counselor stamina. *Journal of Counseling & Development, 82*(3), 319–328.

Reivich, K., & Shatte, A. (2002). *The resilience factor.* New York, NY: Broadway Books.

Rutter, M. (2007). Resilience, competence and coping. *Child Abuse & Neglect, 31*(3), 205–209.

Saleebey, D. (2006). *The strengths perspective in social work practice* (4th ed.). Boston, MA: Allyn and Bacon.

Skovholt, T. M. (2001). *The resilient practitioner: Burnout prevention and self-care strategies for counselors, therapists, teachers, and health professionals.* Boston, MA: Allyn & Bacon.

Taylor, S. E., & Brown, J. D. (1988). Illusion and well-being: A social psychological perspective on mental health. *Psychological Bulletin, 103*, 193–121.

Thieleman, K., & Cacciatore, J. (2014). Witness to suffering: Mindfulness and compassion fatigue among traumatic bereavement volunteers and professionals. *Social Work, 59*(1), 34–41.

Tugade, M., & Fredrickson, B. (2004). Resilient individuals use positive emotions to bounce back from negative emotional experiences. *Journal of Personality and Social Psychology, 86*(2), 320–333.

Wilks, E. S., & Spivey, C. A. (2010). Resilience in undergraduate social work students: Social support and adjustment to academic stress. *Social Work Education, 28*(3), 276–88.

EPILOGUE

The directive is well known. Perhaps as a metaphor, it may even be overused. Even with this as a caveat, the directive remains instructive.

In case of cabinet depressurization, an oxygen mask will descend from the overhead compartment. If traveling with young children, the elderly, or someone needing special assistance (**and here is the important part**), *place the oxygen mask first on yourself and then give assistance to the passenger needing help.*

Put on your mask first!

The directive to care for oneself before assisting another is not only applicable to those within a depressurized cabin but also directly applies to all within the counseling profession. Neglecting his or her physical, emotional, and spiritual health will not only result in a counselor's depleted resources but also render him or her unable to provide the care to the clients the counselor serves. The previous chapters have highlighted both the gift and the cost of serving as a professional counselor. Empathically engaging with another person during times of his or her distress and emotional upset is demanding. Threats of burnout, compassion fatigue, and secondary trauma are real. There are genuinely inherent risks in the work we do, and it is both a practical and ethical responsibility to take the steps necessary to buffer ourselves from these risks, these threats, to our well-being and professional competence.

Self-care is an essential step in this "buffering" process. The concept of self-care and its espoused value is indeed not a foreign concept to counselors. Sadly, however, for too many counselors, self-care is a concept that has applicability only to the "others" with whom they work. Religiously preaching the need and value of self-care is often a process that can be placed into the category of "do as I say, not as I do."

We are not above the damaging effects of stress. We are not immune to emotional and physical exhaustion.

We cannot function without oxygen. We need to "place the mask."

—rdp/kld/ba

INDEX

A

ABC model of wellness, 95–96

Adams, T. B., 90

American Counseling Association (ACA), 2, 5, 48, 63, 70, 75
  Code of Ethics, 5, 24–25
  Task Force on Counselor Wellness and Impairment, 73

American Mental Health Counselors Association (AMHCA), 48

American Psychological Association (APA), 74

American School Counselor Association (ASCA), 5, 12, 25, 48, 70, 75, 84

anxiety, 14

Aponte, H. J., 24

assessment
  burnout, 52–54
  compassion fatigue, 39–42
  wellness orientation, 95

B

Baranowsky, A. B., 34

behavioral symptoms of compassion fatigue, 34

Belton, S., 97

Blount, A. J., 97

Bride, B., 58

burnout, 46–54
  dimensions, 53
  factors contributing to, 50–51
  journey toward, 51–52
  multidimensional, 48–50
  overview, 46–47
  professional mandate, 47–48
  responding to threat of, 52–54

C

Calhoun, L. G., 65

career-sustaining behaviors (CSB), 96–97

Center for Chronic Disease Prevention and Health Promotion, 14

challenges to providing service, 14–15

Christopher, Leo, 80

chronic diseases, 14

Code of Ethics (ACA), 5, 24–25

Code of Ethics (ASCA), 75

cognitive skills, 103–104

commitment to wellness, 96

comorbidity, 14

compassion fatigue, 33–42
  defined, 34
  factors contributing to, 35–37
  impacts of, 36
  personal characteristics, 37
  symptoms, 34, 38–42
  work-related factors, 36

Compassion Fatigue Scale (CFS-R), 39

Compassion Fatigue Self-Test (CFST), 39

compassion satisfaction, 38–42

Corey, Gerald, 5

Counselor Burnout Inventory (CBI), 52–53

counselor preparation program, 85

counselors, 1–7
  challenges to providing service, 14–15
  complex health cases, 13–14
  cycle of caring, 6
  identification, 25–28
  identities, 6–7
  loss of professional objectivity, 23–30
  overview, 1
  professional challenges and gifts, 4–5
  responsibility, 17–18
  role demands, 2–4
  self-care and care of clients, 5–6
  shortages, 12–13

countertransference, 28

creative self-care, 80–86

cycle of caring, 6

D

demand for mental health services, 12–13

depersonalization scale, 52

depression, 14

detachment, 30

deterioration of personal life, 53. *See also* burnout

ABOUT THE AUTHORS

Richard D. Parsons, Ph.D. is a Full Professor in the Counselor Education Department at West Chester University. Dr. Parsons has more than 40 years of university experience teaching in counselor preparation programs. Before his university experience, Dr. Parsons spent 9 years as a school counselor in an inner-city high school. Dr. Parsons has had a private clinical practice for more than 30 years and serves as a consultant to educational institutions and mental health service organizations throughout the tristate area of Pennsylvania, New Jersey, and Delaware, and he has been the recipient of many awards and honors, including the Pennsylvania Counselor of the Year award.

Dr. Parsons has authored or coauthored more than 80 professional articles and books, including *The School Counselor as Consultant: Expanding Impact from Intervention to Prevention* (Cognella Academic Publishing). His most recent books include the series of four training texts for school counselors, *Transforming Theory into Practice* (Corwin Press), and individual texts, including *Becoming a Skilled Counselor, Field Experience and Counseling Theory* (Sage Publications), and *Counseling Strategies That Work! Evidenced-Based Interventions for School Counselors* (Allyn & Bacon).

Karen L. Dickinson, Ph.D. is an Associate Professor in the Department of Counselor Education at West Chester University of Pennsylvania and Graduate Coordinator, having served as the School Counseling Program Coordinator for several years. Dr. Dickinson has more than 10 years of experience teaching at the university level in counseling preparation programs and spent more than 3 decades in the K–12 educational system supporting students as a general education and special education teacher and school counselor.

Dr. Dickinson is the coauthor of *The School Counselor as Consultant: Expanding Impact from Intervention to Prevention* for Cognella Academic Publishing, *A Student's Guide to Handling Stress* for Cognella Academic Publishing, and *Ethical Practice: Beyond Knowing Ethics to Being Ethical* for Sage Publications, as well as a contributing author for *Working with Students with Disabilities*, a text for school counselors, and ancillary author for *Field Experience: Transitioning from Student to Professional*, both for Sage Publications. She has presented nationally and internationally on the topic of bullying and students with disabilities. Other presentations and research focus on the school counselor as an advocate and leader and training the 21st-century school counselor to support diverse student populations.

Bridget Asempapa, Ph.D. is an Assistant Professor in the Department of Counselor Education at West Chester University and the School Counseling Program Coordinator. Dr. Asempapa has a dual license in professional school counseling and clinical mental health counseling. Dr. Asempapa has 3 years of experience in teaching at the university level, including the preparation of counselor education students. Prior to her teaching at the university, she worked with diverse students at the PreK–12 grades in the role of a teacher, school counselor, and as a mental health consultant. Dr. Asempapa has spent seven years working in school systems both at the international and national levels.

Dr. Asempapa's most recent scholarly work focused on developing an instrument (Integrated Care Competency Survey [ICCS]) to measure graduate counseling students' competencies in integrated care. She has authored and coauthored peer-reviewed articles and has presented on various topics at international, national, state, and local conferences. Her research interests include integrated care, adjustment challenges among international students in school counseling, ethical issues in counseling, and challenges in raising children with special needs.

CPSIA information can be obtained
at www.ICGtesting.com
Printed in the USA
LVHW110717101121
702904LV00002B/15

9 781516 593309